FUTURE

Welcome

There's nothing quite so quaint as an English cottage garden, with its chaotic, whimsical charm, low-maintenance upkeep and wildlife-friendly plantings. But it's not simply a case of throwing down seeds and waiting for them to grow. Over the following pages, we'll share the best flowers for your beds, including the traditional rose, as well as foxgloves, delphiniums, geraniums and more. Our experts will talk you through the design rules that every English garden abides to, and how you can make it work in your outdoor space, whatever the size.

Contents

Border design ideas PAGE 48

FEATURES

06 Cottage garden designs
Flowers and scent combine in abundance in this quintessential English garden style

12 Cottage garden essentials
From overflowing borders filled with colourful blooms to pretty accessories and seating that add instant charm, there are many ways to create this garden style

18 50 easy plants for cottage garden style With the right plants, this popular garden look can be achieved in any garden situation

34 Forever green Forming the backbone of the cottage garden, evergreens, with their all-year foliage, should not be overlooked for the potential they offer

48 Design your perfect border
Garden designer Tabi Jackson Gee lays out six border styles that you can plant now to reap the benefits next summer

56 Patio delight
Extend your living space by creating the perfect patio for relaxing, taking inspiration from English cottage gardens for maximum period charm

68 Potted perfection Use a variety of containers to add beautiful highlights to all areas of your cottage garden

74 Container cottage garden
With a little planning, you can create a wonderful floral container display with old-fashioned favourites that evokes the feel of a country cottage garden

86 Clipped to perfection A craft with ancient heritage, topiary can add a magical element to the garden scheme on frosty winter days, and offers all-year interest

98 Small-scale harvesting
No cottage garden is complete without some crops, so if you're short on space, turn to containers, compact beds and vertical surfaces for growing delicious fruit and veg

112 Take control of pests
Don't let the unwanted attention of pests ruin your plant paradise – learn how to identify and limit the impact of common plant predators naturally

Contents

PLANT CARE GUIDES

Our experts reveal the best methods to help these cottage garden staples survive and thrive. For even more growing guides, visit our sister website at www.gardeningetc.com

- 24 **Roses**
- 28 **Clematis**
- 40 **Lavender**
- 44 **Foxgloves**
- 60 **Peonies**
- 64 **Hardy geraniums**
- 78 **Sweet peas**
- 82 **Asters**
- 90 **Hydrangeas**
- 94 **Delphiniums**
- 104 **Cosmos & zinnias**
- 108 **Alliums**
- 122 **Ferns**
- 126 **Dahlias**

Pest control PAGE 112

YOUR GUIDE TO…

- 32 **Perfect pergolas**
  Here's how to train a climber to add romance to your garden

- 38 **Making the cut**
  Take plant cuttings, and fill your borders with infinite blooms

- 55 **Save and sow**
  Harvest seeds from flowers to increase your stock for free

- 72 **Divide and conquer**
  Divide your perennial plants to keep them healthy and bright

English Cottage Gardens Handbook 5

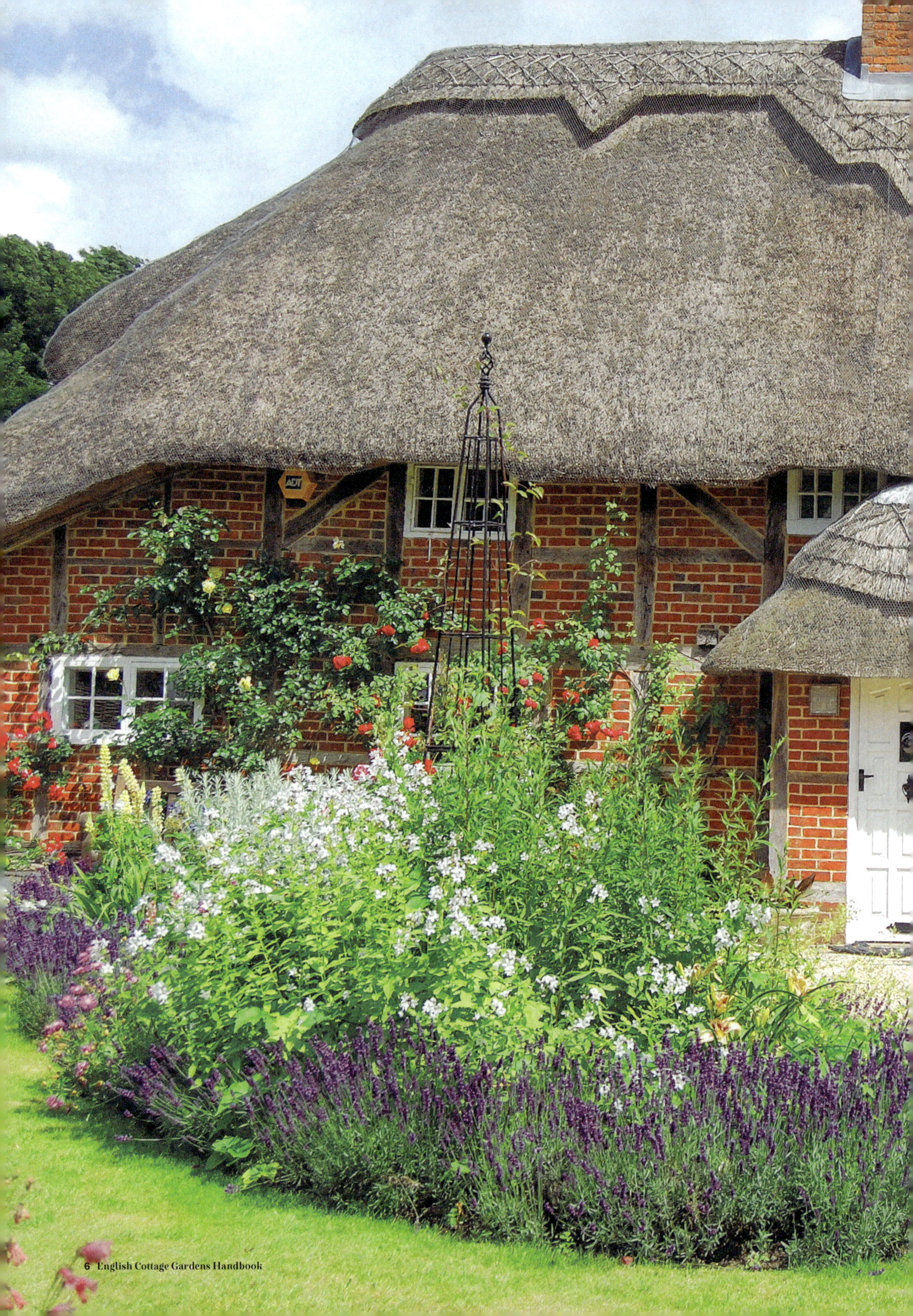
ADT

Cottage garden designs

Cottage garden
designs

Flowers and scents combine in abundance in this quintessential English garden style, with a wide palette planted casually, a little haphazard, and bursting with buzzing wildlife

Words and **photographs**
Leigh Clapp

Soft lines, weathered materials, vintage detailing, heirloom plants and an artless, unstructured look define the cottage garden style – a kaleidoscope of hues and textures from the joyous tangle, as flowers and foliage intermingle and jostle together. 'This is the beautiful chocolate box image everyone has of hollyhocks, roses and colour in a varied tapestry of planting that is very irregular. The use of old-fashioned annuals and even the odd vegetable dotted in as well,' says Rosy Hardy of the renowned Hardy's Cottage Garden Plants.

Traditionally a practical garden, supplying food and medicine around a farm labourer's cottage, the style has evolved and is known and copied across the world as a quintessentially English look. The rather romanticised idea of a country idyll reached a peak in the Victorian times, when the style became more decorative rather than with a productive focus, and was further gentrified by influential designers, such as William Robinson, Gertrude Jekyll and Vita Sackville-West.

This traditional style has remained popular and has become a mix of modern plants and old-fashioned favourites, with an ethos of bio-diversity and a resilient, holistic approach, combining edibles and ornamentals. The striving for sustainability and self-sufficiency echoes the original intent and remains an inspiration.

Designing a cottage garden

Romantic, pretty, effervescent and fun, this is a garden style adaptable for the country, town or city garden, embracing the positive and uplifting joy of flowers and bright colours. There is both a sense of nostalgia and of freedom with a cottage style, which is quite irresistible.

The feel of a cottage garden is relaxed, informal and joyous. There are no strict guidelines or set rules to follow, although, as with any garden, you need to plan the initial layout and planting. Then you are in a partnership with nature, as you can't totally control the evolution of the space, allowing plants to self-seed and become interwoven surprises, with your task that of editing and augmenting as needed.

Plan your scheme for planting in autumn or spring, or buy mature plants at the garden centre or nursery for planting straight away. Perennials and shrubs, for instance, will take root in autumn.

Keep the layout simple, as the infill will be full and busy. Cottage gardens need planning and regular care, so to avoid it from being too labour intensive, start small, with a cottage garden area or border, and then increase the size of your horticultural chocolate box once your confidence grows. You could position this area by a warm and mellow stone wall, behind a picket fence, enclosed by low hedging, or as a pretty confection to greet visitors to your front door.

Think about the hard landscaping, such as paths and focal points. 'A cottage garden should ideally have winding paths, which in midsummer are only just visible between beds bursting with plants. These paths lead your eye to a focal point;

Cottage garden designs

this could be your house, an arbour or even a simple bench,' recommends RHS horticulturalist Catherine Fairhall Lewis, who looks after the ebullient cottage garden at Hyde Hall.

Meandering garden paths of stone, old bricks, gravel or grass offer a visual relief to the exuberance in a larger cottage garden design. Softly curving pathways that blend in are at home in the cottage style, while using reclaimed and natural materials, all contribute to this being one of the most affordable styles.

Planning planting

The mantra 'right plant, right place' is important, as you are working with, not against, your garden's conditions. This will give the healthiest, sturdiest results, with the minimum of effort.

Test your soil so you know which plants are best suited to it and add organic matter, such as compost. Good, rich organic soil, where plants will thrive without too much watering or feeding, will make the job easier, while mulching also helps retain moisture and keep weeds down.

There are plant choices for sun and shade, as well as different soil types, although more will suit sunnier spots. Your aim is for the plants to appear to have planted themselves. 'Plan the position of your big permanent plants – so your trees, roses and shrubs. Smaller flowering perennials will be fitted in the spaces around these, then finally your annuals are used to fill any remaining gaps,' says Catherine. 'When choosing your planting scheme, make sure to include classic cottage garden plants. Be bold with your colours, encourage self-seeding and pack plants closely together so there is no bare earth,' she adds.

Easy-going and easy-care are what you are after, with a mix of tough, reliable perennials and annuals, shrubs for structure, and some bulbs. ▶

Opposite: A rustic lattice divider is covered in cascading rambling roses, but still offers views through to a charming seating area among a floral medley of poppies and lupins
Right: Storybook hollyhocks frame a sun-loving mix of daisies, salvias, campanula, evening primroses and eryngium
Below: Poppies and aquilegia daintily fringe a meandering stone path, accompanied by easy-care euphorbias, Centranthus ruber, Stachys byzantina and shrub roses

The top five cottage garden plants recommended by the RHS for 'voluptuous planting and haphazard self-seeding' are foxgloves, lavender, delphiniums, scented philadelphus and roses. Add to your palette with others that also epitomise the cottage garden look, such as nepeta, hollyhocks, phlox, hardy geraniums, love-in-a-mist, stocks, dianthus, cosmos, peonies, sweet peas, aquilegia, daisies of all kinds, and wildflowers.

Plant more closely than you would normally so everything knits together with a blousy effect. 'Include plants that flower repeatedly, really earning their place when space is limited,' suggests Rosy Hardy.

'Examples that you can plant include *Geranium* 'Rozanne', as it flowers from June to October; *Nepeta grandiflora* 'Summer Magic', which can be grown as edging or as a substitute for a lavender hedge in soils where lavender does not thrive; *Geum* 'Totally Tangerine' whose soft tangerine flowers dance on fuzzy stems and is one of the longest flowering perennials at the nursery; and one of our own, the very delicate ruffled semi-double *Anemone* 'Frilly Knickers', which won HTA Virtual Plant Awards 2020,' Rosy explains.

Feature focus

Ornaments, such as a rustic birdbath, sundial or seat, add focus among the planting profusion, helping to break up the intensity of the planting and provide a place to rest the eye.

Upcycling, recycling and vintage finds fit the cottage garden style, but use these additions in moderation. Ideas for recycled or vintage items you could incorporate include an old wheelbarrow billowing with flowers; moss-covered statuary; stone finials half-buried in plantings; tools made into sculptures, or planted rustic troughs.

Add height or focal points with romantic arbours, arches, pergolas or obelisks draped in scented climbers, such as roses, honeysuckle or jasmine. Again use these items with consideration so the whole effect doesn't become too hectic.

As with all elements of the cottage garden, however, it is an opportunity to express your own personal taste, so feel free to do what appeals to you. There are no rules.

Get the cottage garden look

- No social-distancing in this style – instead it is all about informal crowding. This is an ideal style for the self-confessed plantaholic
- Ensure every piece of ground is covered in an apparently unstructured design
- Use high-performance, tough plants – such as non-hybridised flowers that appeal to pollinators
- Select disease-resistant shrub roses and ramblers
- Don't forget interesting foliage from choices such as *Stachys byzantina*, *Alchemilla mollis* and ornamental grasses
- Fragrance is a feature of many favourite old-fashioned cottage plants
- Select a colour palette that appeals to you and works with the architecture of your home – this can be from soft and pastel, dreamy and romantic, to vibrant and clashing
- Include some hidden surprises to discover
- Trim and tidy new growth, and deadhead flowers to keep the show going for as long as possible
- Add in some productive plants among the floral profusion, such as a self-fertile dwarf fruit tree, vegetables and herbs

The cottage garden style is an economical design, so grow flowers from seed, such as inexpensive annuals, take cuttings, allow self-seeders to spread, and if something pops up in the wrong spot, dig it up and move it.

Below left to right: Have fun repurposing vintage salvage into containers or sculptural detail among the profusion of blooms in bed and borders; foxgloves are synonymous with the cottage garden look and there are many varieties to choose from; stately delphiniums will grace the garden through summer – cut them to the ground after the first flowering and they will give you a second flush come August; woven willow supports are a perfect choice for delicate and fragrant sweet peas

Above: A sundial focal point rests the eye among the ebullient tapestry of colours and textures, from deep burgundy Dahlia 'Nuit d'Eté', frothy Ammi majus, euphorbia, salvias, alstroemeria and roses

Ready cottage garden recipes

SHAKE AND SOW, COTTAGE GARDENS – RHS box of seeds, with traditional mix of cottage garden favourites. Contains flowers for cutting and will provide a food source for birds and beneficial insects. Sow April to June, flowers June to October (rhsplants.co.uk)
COTTAGE GARDEN PERENNIAL COLLECTION – selection to attract butterflies and bees. Includes delphiniums, lupins, foxgloves, echinacea, hollyhocks, module plants. Flowers summer to autumn (jparkers.co.uk)
READY-MADE COTTAGE GARDEN SCHEME – for a sunny summer border, 2m x 4m. 34 plants available, including grasses, lavender, campanula, phlox and chives (crocus.co.uk)
BORDER IN A BOX – English cottage garden design, includes labelled garden design, plant list, seeds for between plants, care and flowering information (borderinabox.com)
GARDEN ON A ROLL – English cottage border shrubs and perennials (gardenonaroll.com)

Plant sources

HARDY'S COTTAGE GARDEN PLANTS, Hants RG28 7FA (Tel: 01256 896533; hardysplants.co.uk)
SARAH RAVEN, East Sussex TN32 5HP (Tel: 0345 092 0283; sarahraven.com)
BLUEBELL COTTAGE GARDENS NURSERY, Cheshire WA4 4HP (Tel: 01928 713718; bluebellcottage.co.uk)
PEAK COTTAGE PLANTS, Derbyshire DE4 2DH (Tel: 01629 650428; peakcottageplants.co.uk) ●

Gardens to visit

RHS GARDEN HYDE HALL, Chelmsford CM3 8ET. The gardens include large cottage beds overflowing with romantic, informal, colourful blooms, from flowers, shrubs, fruit trees and the odd vegetable. Open daily, 10am–6pm. Entry adult £12.15, child £6.10. Tel: 01245 402019; rhs.org.uk
ANNE HATHAWAY'S COTTAGE, Stratford-upon-Avon CV37 9HH. Picture-book thatched cottage with perennials, productive patch and wildflower orchard. Open Saturday–Wednesday, 10am–4pm. Entry adult £15, child £10.50. Tel: 01789 204016; shakespeare.org.uk
EAST LAMBROOK MANOR GARDENS, South Petherton TA13 5HH. Contemporary approach to cottage planting. Open Tuesday–Saturday, 10am–5pm. Entry adult £6.50, child free. Tel: 01460 240 328; eastlambrook.com

Cottage garden essentials

From overflowing borders filled with colourful blooms to pretty accessories and seating that add instant charm, there are many ways to create this garden style

Words Holly Crossley & Rachel Crow

Above: Punctuate hard landscaping in a cottage garden with terracotta containers brimming with soft and fragrant colourful blooms

Romantic and whimsical, with voluptuous borders full of colour and texture, amid traditional hard landscaping materials, cottage gardens are beautiful spaces packed with soft flowers and scent.

Traditionally, they would have been full of edible plants, but while you can still find ornamental vegetables in cottage-style borders, in today's interpretation, flowers steal the show. Guided by nature, full of self-seeding plants, tumbling blooms and rambling vines, a cottage garden requires more editing than planting.

You don't have to live in a picture-postcard thatched cottage in the countryside to embrace this garden style, either. The look can work just as well on a smaller scale in a flower-filled urban plot. Disguise hard landscaping behind foliage, succulents, moss and tumbling flowers to create this naturalistic, carefree appeal.

While the overall result tends to err on the informal, that doesn't mean that the layout should not be considered. Large borders and winding pathways are the epitome of a cottage garden style, but there is a fine line between wonderfully rambling and simply chaotic.

Start with a plan – decide where your borders will be located, and what shape they will be, and then augment with some of these cottage garden ideas for the perfect plot.

Cottage garden essentials

Natural embrace

'One of the most wonderful things about the cottage style of gardening is that it was borne out of the need to do things cheaply and simply. Materials for paths and walls look better if they are reclaimed and reused, which can be a great money saver as well as being better for the environment,' explains garden designer Tracy Foster. 'Brick edges, simple gravel paths, paving with self-seeded herbs and flowers growing in the cracks, or stepping stones running through planting, are some examples.

'Anything that looks handcrafted or homemade will fit in well, such as woven willow obelisks, cleft chestnut fencing or hazel hurdles,' Tracy adds.

Meadow dreams

Historically, the quintessential cottage garden would have evolved slowly and planting would have had no strict plan. Self-seeders were welcomed and new plants were propagated from cuttings. They would have also been gifted by neighbours and perhaps collected from the native countryside. All flowers would have been planted in whatever space was available, with little thought to hierarchy or height, which resulted in a magical jumble of shape and colour.

Although colour blocking is a great way to create cohesion and impact, if you are seeking a wild meadow feel, layer up a variety of hues and heights for a more natural result. ➤

Mellow brick walls and gravel paths are among the material choices

Layer swathes of planting for an abundant, meadow feel

English Cottage Gardens Handbook **13**

Edible elements

The purpose of the cottage garden was traditionally to grow vegetables, such as peas, beans, cabbages, onions, leeks and carrots, but also a wide array of herbs that would have been used in cooking, for medicinal purposes as well as for household uses.

Grow edibles among the ornamentals in beds and borders, such as pretty, frilly-leafed lollo rosso, or a cane wigwam supporting clambering runner beans. If you have the luxury of more space, create dedicated raised garden beds for growing herbs and vegetable and fruit crops in a sunny, south-facing area of the garden, which will be alive and buzzing with beneficial pollinators.

Under glass

As a cottage garden requires an abundance of blooms, the most cost-effective way to fill borders with flowers is to grow plants from seed. Including space for a greenhouse – or even a cold frame, if room is limited – can bring many benefits. Much like cottage gardens, 'greenhouses are intrinsically linked to a romantic, comforting notion of Englishness,' says Martin Toogood, chairman of glasshouse manufacturer Hartley Botanic.

As we enter summer, greenhouses can take on a multifunctional purpose in a cottage garden. More than just a growing space, a greenhouse can also offer somewhere to sit and enjoy spending time immersed among the plants.

Create a kitchen garden area or plant edibles among flowers

A greenhouse will prove invaluable for raising flower and crop seedlings

Cottage garden essentials

Head for heights

Whatever the garden style, always consider the vertical space. Using plants and features of different heights helps to create interest at all levels for a fuller, more impactful display.

Trellis, wooden arbours, or obelisks can support climbing plants – whether placed in a large container, beside garden walls, or among other blooms in a deep border – while a pergola can provide height and character.

Arbours and pergolas are also useful for framing a point in your path to help divide areas of the garden. Train floriferous and fragrant climbers to scramble up them, from climbing roses to clematis and honeysuckle. Wooden structures can also be painted to complement the garden colour scheme. ➤

Nepeta and Alchemilla mollis make a lovely pairing for massed perennial planting

Softly curving beds and borders lend the garden design a more informal feel, and winding paths invoke a childlike sense of wonder and adventure

Perennial pleasure

There are many perennials that make perfect choices for low-maintenance, cottage-style borders. 'Although you may be tempted to fill it with every plant you can find, it might be wise to hold back ever so slightly. Make a list of the plants you most want,' says garden designer Fi Boyle. 'It is definitely best to limit the palette. By having groups of the same plant repeated through a border you create a rhythm that helps the border to hang together and feel less busy,' she adds.

Perennials such as scabious, penstemons, nepeta and *Alchemilla mollis* will come back year after year, while hardy geraniums are available in a wide range of varieties. No cottage garden would also be complete without roses, whether climbing or rambling, softening walls or fences.

Soft curves

While formal gardens were laid out with parterres and terraces, traditional cottage garden layouts were much less predetermined. 'The look lends itself well to narrow paths and flowing curves,' says designer Tracy Foster.

To capture the romance of a classic cottage garden, try to avoid straight lines and instead, factor in plenty of deep, curved borders for planting. Curved landscaping always creates a more natural and relaxed feel that allows you to meander along pathways through the flower beds. ●

Cottage garden essentials

Planted profusion

Even the smallest courtyard can be transformed into a whimsical haven of colour and texture. Train climbers to clamber up surfaces, and fill terracotta pots with your favourite cottage garden perennials, or create miniature meadow scenes with the likes of cosmos, cornflowers, poppies, zinnias, pincushion flowers or ox-eye daisies. Dot around all levels of your patio space for a gorgeous display.

Don't be afraid to welcome a touch of the wild by allowing nature to do its thing, with moss, lichen or seedlings popping up between, or forming a living carpet over patio stones. The rusted patination of quaint wrought-iron chairs and tables can transport you straight to Frances Hodgson Burnett's *The Secret Garden*.

50 EASY PLANTS FOR Cottage garden *style*

With the right plants, this popular garden look can be achieved in just about any garden situation

50 easy plants for cottage gardens

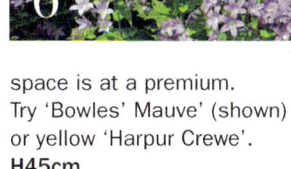

SMALL GARDEN CHOICES

Choose plants that flower for a long period or have more than one season to maintain interest in a small plot

1 FOXGLOVE
Grown in cottage gardens for centuries, these bell-shaped flowers are loved by bees. Cut the main spike as it fades and more will come. It likes shade and is self-seeding. **H1.5m**

2 ORNAMENTAL QUINCE
Chaenomeles flowers in spring, with large, round fruits in autumn. Train against a wall and prune after flowering. Try 'Apple Blossom'. **H1.5m**

3 PERENNIAL WALLFLOWER
A great cottage garden favourite, this perennial wallflower is useful where space is at a premium. Try 'Bowles' Mauve' (shown) or yellow 'Harpur Crewe'. **H45cm**

4 WINTER CLEMATIS
The variety *C. cirrhosa* var. *balearica* 'Freckles' has ferny foliage and produces beautiful scented spotted bell flowers in late winter. Train up a sheltered wall or fence. **H2.4m**

5 FRENCH LAVENDER
Aromatic leaves and spikes of tufted flowers. Thrives in a warm spot in full sun, and must have free-draining soil to survive winter. **H50cm**

6 CAMPANULA LACTIFLORA
Its upright form is a must-have for a small cottage border. Blue starry bells appear from mid-summer to autumn. Try 'Prichard's Variety' (shown). Full sun or part shade. **H75cm**

Top tip For impact, plant in repeating drifts

FOR RESTRICTED BUDGETS

Great-value plants are those that are inexpensive, easy to grow and propagate, and give months of pleasure all summer

7 ROSE
No cottage garden is complete without roses. Choose a repeat-flowering shrub rose that holds the prestigious RHS Award of Garden Merit for ease of maintenance, such as 'Cornelia' (shown). **H1.5m**

8 ALCHEMILLA MOLLIS
This perennial is ideal for edging borders and planting beneath shrubs. A froth of lime-green flowers contrast with roses. Propagate by division; it self-seeds. **H45cm**

9 STACHYS BYZANTINA
Called lamb's ears, this plant, with its soft, hairy evergreen leaves, forms a useful weed barrier and is a great companion to roses. Spikes of purple flowers appear in summer. Propagate by division; plant in full sun. **H50cm** ➤

English Cottage Gardens Handbook 19

FOR SUNNY GARDENS

A dreamy cottage garden is filled with colour and is rich with different plants mingling among shrubs which help create a sense of proportion

10 LUPIN
No cottage garden setting is complete without spires of lupins. Position in full sun and cut fading flower spikes near the base to encourage a second flush. Team up with pretty geraniums (cranesbills). **H1.2m**

11 GERANIUM 'ROZANNE'
A very easy-to-grow geranium (cranesbill), this makes a good companion to lupins in May and June. An ideal gap filler, trim after flowering. Propagate by dividing plants in spring. **H60cm**

12 ASTRANTIA
A sumptuous perennial and old cottage favourite for the middle of the border. Look for the variety 'Gill Richardson' which has beautiful burgundy flowers. Astrantias prefer a well drained yet moist soil. **H75cm**

13 CALENDULA
A well-known annual to light up the garden in summer with brilliant-orange or yellow flowers. Sow the seed in their final positions outdoors and allow some to set seed for a repeat performance. **H50cm**

14 CISTUS
Best in a dry soil and full sun, the rock rose is a pretty evergreen. The variety 'Grayswood Pink' has a spreading habit and makes a good ground-cover plant. Take cuttings in summer. **H1m**

15 DAHLIA
For a modern feel, choose purple or black-leaved dahlias, such as the 'Bishop' varieties. Most have single flowers, are good for pollinators and are great cutting flowers. **H90cm**

16 ECHINACEA
Striking large daisy flowers in shades of purplish pink, white and even yellow. Like all coneflowers, the hybrid 'Robert Bloom' is loved by bees and butterflies. **H1.2m**

> **Top tip** Incorporate lots of organic matter in soil in dry shade your borders

> **Top tip** Make sure tall plants are staked

FOR SHADE

Most gardens have a shady side; use this area as a chance to incorporate interesting plant combinations

17 PULMONARIA
Lungwort brightens a shaded border. Leaf markings vary from spotted, silver or variegated, while spring flowers open pink and change to blue. **H50cm**

18 SOFT SHIELD FERN
Add an informal cottage feel to a shady spot with the fresh unfurling fronds of the evergreen shield fern (*Polystichum setiferum*). **H1.5m**

19 DICENTRA
Transforms a dull corner in spring, with arching stems of white or rose-pink flowers. Plant in a moist soil in semi-shade.

EDIBLES

Traditional cottage gardening mixes fruit and vegetables with flowers and herbs. This encourages pest predators and creates a healthy, balanced environment

Top tip
Grow small patches of edible plants at the front of your borders

22 REDCURRANT
Heavy cropping and easy to grow, redcurrants thrive in shady sites where other crops struggle. Enjoy the fruits fresh or make jams. **H1.5m**

23 COURGETTE
Sow two seeds per pot March to April, harden off and plant out after the last frost. Try 'Defender' with resistance to diseases or yellow 'Soleil'. Water well in hot spells. **H60cm**

24 APPLE
The eventual size of an apple tree is determined by its rootstock. 'Step Over' M27 trees are supplied trained in a horizontal tier low to the ground. Use as edging for flower beds. **H45-60cm**

25 STRAWBERRY
Strawberries look lovely at the edge of containers where fruits tumble over the sides. Tasty alpine strawberries are easy to grow from seed and these prefer a shady spot in pots and borders. **H15cm**

Plants die down after flowering only to return the following year. **H1.2m**

20 JAPANESE HONEYSUCKLE
A twining honeysuckle that will grow in sunshine or shade. It produces glorious fragrant white flowers in summer that age to yellow. Look for *Lonicera japonica* 'Halliana'. **H4-8m**

21 ERYTHRONIUM DENS-CANIS
Attractive mottled leaves and single flowers with swept-back petals appear in spring. Best planted in drifts, dog's-tooth violets are easy to grow in moist shady borders. **H20cm**

FOR LAID-BACK GARDENERS

Reduce the workload of a cottage garden with resilient plants that do not need regular watering or pruning

26 HUMULUS LUPULUS
This hop thrives given an obelisk or trellis for support. Attractive hanging clusters of flowers appear in late summer. Take cuttings in summer. **H8m**

27 SEDUM
The ice plant 'Purple Emperor' (shown) comes into its own in late summer when deep-pink flowers are magnets for butterflies and bees. Prefers free-draining soil. **H60cm**

28 HELICTOTRICHON SEMPERVIRENS
The evergreen blue oat grass has tall spikes with purple-flecked flowers. Ideal for a gravel border or prairie-style planting with sedums. Trim in early spring. **H1.2m** ➤

English Cottage Gardens Handbook 21

Top tip
The larger the container, the less often you need to water it

DROUGHT-TOLERANT

As our summers get warmer it makes sense to incorporate garden plants that are resistant to drought. Choose those that originate from hot, dry places and are adapted to such conditions

tolerant. Cut back to almost ground level in spring. **H45cm**

31 MARGUERITES
Cut these cottage favourites back in the growing season to promote flowering. **H45cm**

32 COSMOS
Pink blooms with feathery foliage. For pots, choose dwarf 'Sonata Carmine'. **H45cm-1.5m**

33 TULIPS
There are hundreds of tulip varieties to choose from. 'Black Parrot' (shown) is particularly glamorous. **H45cm**

34 PENNISETUMS
Mulch fountain grass to protect roots in autumn. Cut back stems in spring. **H80cm**

35 SUNFLOWERS
Reliable in pots but protect from slugs. Go for dwarf types such as 'Teddy Bear' (shown). **H60cm**

36 VERBASCUM PHOENICEUM
Copes well in poor soil but extra-fertile conditions will allow plants to put on more vigorous growth. Flowers vary in colour from white to pink to dark purple. Try the pretty 'Southern Charm'. **H1.2m**

37 GAZANIAS
These jewel-bright plants are perfect for a hot, dry position. They come in a range of vivid orange, golden-yellow or pink flowers that open fully when the sun shines. **H25cm**

38 SISYRINCHIUM 'CALIFORNIA SKIES'
A relative of the iris with dainty starry flowers which appear above strappy foliage all summer. Versatile in any situation in sun or partial shade and unfussy about soil. **H20cm**

39 ERIGERON KARVINSKIANUS
The Mexican fleabane quickly forms a carpet of green leaves that becomes studded with thousands of white daisies ageing to pink. This plant does well growing in gaps in between paving. **H15cm**

40 SALVIA PATENS
Gentian sage thrives in hot sun in a sheltered spot with well-drained soil. Watch out for slug and snail damage in spring. Take cuttings to get even more plants next year. **H60cm**

BASKETS AND POTS

Makes sure your pots and containers are overflowing with soft, generous flowers

29 CINERARIA 'SILVER DUST'
With its mat of felty silver leaves, this is the perfect filler plant between annuals. Prune lightly to keep compact. **H25cm**

30 COREOPSIS
Delightful golden daisies with fringed edges, ideal for containers. They are drought

22 English Cottage Gardens Handbook

50 easy plants for cottage gardens

FOCAL POINTS
Every garden benefits from eye-catching plants that make good focal points; something surprisingly different from neighbouring plants and which seizes your attention

47 *ILEX* 'GOLDEN KING'
Holly clipped into lollipop shapes creates a distinctive structure which offsets the natural effect of the rest of the planting. In winter the holly will become the main feature.

48 SWEET PEAS
Grow this climbing annual up a wigwam frame and pick blooms often to encourage more. Sow in pots in October or spring and transplant one plant per cane in May. **H2m**

49 *ACER PALMATUM*
Graceful Japanese maples have finely cut leaves that turn spectacular colours in autumn. Although slow growing, consider the eventual height when choosing. **H6m**

50 WEEPING PEAR
A beautiful ornamental tree, *Pyrus salicifolia* 'Pendula' is clothed in grey downy leaves and creamy-white flowers in spring. It makes an attractive focal point. Happy in well-drained soil in full sun. **H5m**

44 LILIES
The pure-white 'Casa Blanca' like many of the Oriental lilies will create a spectacular display in pots. Try *Lilium regale* with elongated trumpets on tall stems. Lilies enjoy full sun with roots in the shade. **H1.2m**

45 STOCKS
Matthiola incana is an annual easily grown from seed. Pinch out the tops to encourage branching. As a cut flower, remove all the leaves below the water line. **H40cm**

46 ALSTROEMERIAS
Colours range from rich orange and burgundy tones, to delicate green-splashed 'Blushing Bride' (shown). To protect the crowns from frost, add a deep layer of bark in autumn. **H60cm**

CUTTING GARDEN
There's nothing like growing your own flowers for cutting and displaying indoors

41 SWEET WILLIAM
An easy-to-grow cottage garden favourite with spicy-scented flowers in summer. Prefers a sunny spot and tolerates most soils. **60cm**

42 *ORLAYA GRANDIFLORA*
A great-value annual with a long show of lacy white umbels. Sow seed in September where they are to flower or start off in pots in spring. **H75cm**

43 CORNFLOWERS
Start off seed in spring for late-summer flowers the next year. 'Black Ball' lasts well in a vase and dries without fading; keep picking to encourage more blooms. Full sun. **H1.2m**

Top tip — Grow flowers in rows in your cutting garden for easy picking

English Cottage Gardens Handbook 23

Roses

Romance of the rose

The queen of flowers is a beautiful, fragrant and colourful addition to gardens of all sizes and styles. Learn how to grow them with our guide

Words and **photographs** Leigh Clapp

Roses are an icon of the English garden; they offer such beauty of colour, shape and fragrance, whether entwining with clematis around an arbour, mixed in a herbaceous border, or sprawling over a fence. Roses are versatile for both formal and informal styles, making them a gorgeous addition to any garden.

Types of roses

Species or **wild** roses like to sprawl in a natural style, are mostly single-flowered, and many have colourful hips in autumn, such as rugosa, glauca, moyesii and canina.

Roses from before 1860 are known as **old garden** roses and are characterised by large, graceful shrubs with mostly one flowering, are richly fragrant and include alba, gallica, damask, cabbage and moss roses.

Modern roses, bred from the early 20th century, have characteristics of repeat-flowering and a striving for disease resistance, vigour and flower quality. These cover hybrid teas, floribundas, landscape, climbers, miniature and David Austin English roses.

To add a little confusion, the diverse and versatile **shrub** roses don't fit any distinct classification. They can be wild rose species and also hybrids, taking the best of the old, combined with modern traits of repeat-flowering and diversity of form, colour and fragrance.

When to plant

Late autumn is a great time to plant bare-root roses – the most economical option. Don't plant when the ground is frozen in mid-winter, although you can also plant late winter to early spring. Container-grown roses can be planted year round, except when the soil is frozen, waterlogged, or during periods of drought.

Perfect position

With their wide variety of colours, sizes and growth habits there are rose choices for practically any garden setting. They can be grown in dedicated beds, among other plants in borders, draped over arches and walls, trained around a door, used as groundcover or varieties selected for containers.

Roses are sun-loving plants, preferring from six to eight hours of sun a day. They like well-drained soil that still holds moisture long enough for the roots to absorb it – incorporate some well-rotted compost or manure at planting. Ideally they prefer a soil pH of 6.5, with a heavy loam soil. Too much clay can cause waterlogged roots and sandy soil will drain too freely before the nutrients can be absorbed. If you have dense clay, adding some compost, composted manure or leaf mould will loosen it. There are some really tough roses that cope with a range of conditions, including rugosa and some vigorous cultivars. Some varieties, such as floribunda and shrub roses, can tolerate shade, as long as it isn't caused by trees, so do check the details carefully for shade tolerance. Don't plant roses in exposed locations as wind can both damage blooms and cause evaporation of moisture from foliage. Plant about one metre from other plants to avoid competition and about 60cm from another rose.

Right: The richly toned deep orange splashed with red buds of the repeat-flowering English rose, 'Lady of Shallot' open to a soft apricot salmon hue, with the fragrance described as warm tea with hints of spiced apple and cloves – quite delicious

Romance of the rose

Classic containers

Patio and miniature rose varieties are ideal for containers. English roses also work well with their rounded, bushy shapes; standard roses are elegant options, and ground-covering roses and shorter climbers can also be used. Ensure the container is large enough for your choice – around 10 to 15 litres for small roses, at least 25 litres for English roses and larger for climbers. Select a loam based compost, water regularly, feed through summer and top dress every other year. Re-pot shrub and climbing roses every few years into larger pots.

How to care for roses

Watering is important until the rose is established and then these deep-rooted plants can survive on the natural moisture in the soil. If you do need to water your roses, do so in the morning and aim for their roots, not the leaves.

'I believe the best practice for optimal healthy ➤

roses is to be as eco-friendly as possible as well as choosing the best and healthiest varieties available,' explains Harry Baldwin, head of horticulture at Borde Hill Garden in Sussex.

'Each winter, after pruning in January, we lay a thick layer of well rotted horse manure, which not only supplies the roses with important nutrients but also ensures moisture is retained in the soil preventing unnecessary watering during the summer. The roses also have seaweed foliage feed monthly during the summer,' adds Harry.

Deadhead any spent blooms unless you also want the rose hips, as setting seed saps energy for flower production. Prune the plants in February or March with clean, sharp secateurs when they are bare of leaves.

'For correct pruning, check which rose group they are as this will differ. The principles are the same, however: remove dead, diseased and dying wood first, then open up the centre of the bush as this will help with airflow to reduce potential issues with black spot,' explains Jon Webster, curator at RHS Garden Rosemoor.

The general aim with pruning is to reduce the size of bush roses by around a third, give groundcover roses a light trim, and cut back climbing roses after flowering to suit the structure they are covering.

David Austin Roses are designed to be very forgiving, if you are new to pruning, and they need to be cut to about half their size, creating a rounded shape. Wild roses, such as the rugosas, need no annual pruning, just cut away the dead branches from the underside of the shrub every few years.

Troubleshooting

Fungal diseases, such as black spot, can be a problem with the older types of roses. 'Where possible, buy disease-resistant varieties; this will help to limit the threat of the dreaded black spot,' says Jon Webster. Prevention is always better than cure, so maintaining the health of your roses is key. 'Keeping them full of vigour and growth will also help them as they are hungry plants. After pruning, apply a general-purpose or rose fertiliser followed by a mulch of well-rotted manure. Throughout the growing season the use of a product such as SB Plant Invigorator, which is a bio-stimulant and contains natural elements, such as seaweed, will help to stimulate plant growth; it can also control powdery mildew and aphids,' Jon adds.

Aphids are a common pest and can be hosed off, squashed in your fingers or you could use a spray. Attracting some ladybirds with companion planting will also help. Roses in containers are more susceptible to aphids, so keep an eye out and remove them before they get to colony state. Other pests include caterpillars, sawfly, thrips and red spider mite – attract natural predators with companion planting before reaching for a spray.

Root decay can occur from diseases such as honey fungus, if the plant is waterlogged. Don't plant roses where they have recently grown to avoid replant disorder. 'To overcome this it is best to choose new ground for the roses. If this is not possible to do, adopt a combined strategy of soil exchange and the use of Mycorrhizal fungi to aid their establishment,' suggests Jon Webster.

Good companions

Roses don't like to be crowded or compete for nutrients, but look wonderful mingling with an array of plants. Think of when the roses will be in bloom and also when you will need to camouflage bare stems.

'Despite roses being the real spotlight at Borde Hill, we feel additional plant companions not only extend the season or colour, but also draw more insect predators, helping to keep pests under control. Nepeta and lavender do just that – they open a sea of blue flowers, providing an early display while attracting a wealth of insects, including bees, hoverflies and ladybirds,' says Harry Baldwin.

At the National Trust's Mottisfont, they use a huge range of companion planting, including herbaceous perennials, bulbs and annuals to help showcase the National Collection of pre-1900 shrub roses. 'I think the plants that really epitomise Mottisfont are the tall spires of white foxgloves bringing height to the display; soft blue and white campanulas and geraniums contrasting with the pink and purple gallica roses; and the low-lying, sweetly scented dianthus, which provide an understory to the shrubs at the front of the border,' says gardener Victoria Escourt.

Classic rose companion combinations include cottage garden favourites, such as peonies, campanula, lupins, delphiniums, clematis and geraniums. For bedding plants around roses, use low-growing choices such as alyssum, erigeron, bulbs and *Alchemilla mollis*.

SOURCES FOR ROSES
BRITISH ROSES – britishroses.co.uk
DAVID AUSTIN ROSES – davidaustinroses.co.uk
HARKNESS ROSES – roses.co.uk
PETER BEALES ROSES – classicroses.co.uk
WORLD OF ROSES – worldofroses.com ●

Right: With an absolute profusion of dainty semi-double pink to white flowers, 'Adélaïde D'Orléans' is a wonderful rambler for a fragrant summer tunnel of beauty. Train it to scramble up a pergola covering a walkway to create a magical journey

Romance of the rose

RECOMMENDED VARIETIES

Rosa 'Ballerina' – Small shrub with sprays of pink and white blooms

Rosa 'Blue for You' – Semi-double, sweetly scented violet flowers

Rosa 'Leander' – Tall shrub or climber with fragrant apricot flowers

Rosa 'Graham Thomas' – Cupped blooms of rich, pure yellow

Rosa 'Duchess of Cornwall' – Old-fashioned cupped orangey-pink blooms

Rosa 'Flower Carpet Pink Supreme' – Groundcover with clusters

Rosa 'Munstead Wood' – Velvety deep crimson with fruity fragrance

Rosa 'Jacqueline Du Pre' – Semi-double, blush-white with pink stamens

Rosa 'Ghislaine de Féligonde' – Repeat-flowering musk rambler

English Cottage Gardens Handbook 27

Clematis

All entwined

Plants that grow on vertical structures are useful for bringing beauty to a different dimension – adding height, acting as camouflage, creating shade, providing privacy or adding scent on another level – and queen of the climbers is clematis

Words and **photographs** Leigh Clapp

Climbers, vines or creepers are plants that naturally grow on vertical structures through their ability to sucker or entwine with stems and tendrils. They are an important feature and can be used in a variety of ways, from scrambling over a pergola or archway and clothing a trellis or fence to wandering through trees. Climbers are particularly valuable in small gardens as they take up little ground space and can be grown in containers. By covering surfaces they provide shelter for insects and sometimes birds, and many of the flowers attract pollinators, too.

'There is nearly an endless choice of climbers, so there is a plant for all occasions, able to suit any aspect or style,' says Jack Aldridge, horticulturalist at RHS Garden Wisley, a woody plant enthusiast with a keen interest in climbers.

The popular, showy and perennial clematis offer a wide range from which to select, with varying flower sizes and shapes, from tiny bells to large dinner plates, myriad colours, and different flowering times. Grown mostly for their blooms, some can be in flower 10 months of the year while there are others that only bloom once. Flowering periods differ with winter and spring, early summer, and late summer and autumn. Size is also a key factor as herbaceous clematis grow to between 75cm and 1.5m tall – some are very vigorous, while others are smaller and more compact.

The best way to grow

Clematis can transform an outdoor space of any size, adorning fences, walls, arches, obelisks or tunnels, scrambling up trees or winding their way through other plants. Herbaceous clematis are grown through plant supports or nearby shrubs while climbing types need a trellis or wire attached to the surface with a gap of about 2.5cm.

Viticella varieties are easy to start with, have a great colour range, tolerate different locations and enjoy a long flowering period. Consider the space you want them to cover to help with your selection and then choose the colours you like. Some could be too vigorous and become a nuisance in a small space.

When and where to plant

Spring or early to mid-autumn are the best times to plant clematis. If you buy them in containers through summer, plant them out immediately.

Clematis like their roots in the shade and top growth in the sun. 'Don't grow clematis on a south-facing wall; the base of the wall must have a cool root system,' advises world-renowned clematis grower and breeder Raymond Evison.

'Clematis also need the micro-climate from other plants, formed by growing through another shrub, such as a rose, which will give a burst of flowering at the same time. I like them in herbaceous borders and letting them run up into other plant material. Take a look at your borders in August and note any gaps,' Raymond adds.

They need moisture-retentive, well-drained, fertile soil, in a sunny spot, although there are some varieties that tolerate shade. Add plenty of organic matter when planting and ensure that the top of its roots are 5-6cm deeper than when it was growing in the nursery pot.

How to grow in containers

Clematis grow well in pots and there are varieties ➤

All entwined

Clockwise from top left: These attractive painted obelisk supports echo the pair of conifers that also draw the eye in this flower and edibles formal garden. You could have all the same variety of clematis or choose different ones that harmonise or contrast; clematis casually climbing through an apple tree is charming in a cottage garden among a medley of foliage and flowers; orchestrated roses, clematis and perennials create a rhythm along the flint wall, each colour richly harmonious in a classic scheme of pinks, blues and purples; choose two varieties for double the impact; swathed as a curtain to frame the mirror gives the illusion of looking through a window in this lovely vignette

such as the Boulevard Series that are especially bred to be more compact in their habit, longer flowering and easier to prune – you'll just need to remove the top growth at the end of February to early March.

'Select the strong, dark colours such as deep reds, dark blues, purples and whites for sunny positions, while for shadier places or a patio garden opt for pale pinks, pale blues and mauve flowered options,' recommends Raymond.

Use pots that are at least 45cm wide and deep, have good drainage, and potting on compost, like John Innes No.2 or 3. Avoid plastic or thin-walled pots, as they will heat up too much in summer.

'Make sure that the container is kept well watered through spring and summer and the plant has a shady root system. Clematis are boring in winter, so partner with shallow-rooted bedding or low-growing plants such as ajuga, and early bulbs to give interest and colour,' Raymond continues.

How to care for clematis

They are thirsty and hungry plants, so water regularly until established and feed them a tomato or rose fertiliser during the peak spring and early summer months. Guiding stems to spread evenly over their support can help flowering.

When it comes to pruning, clematis are divided into three groups:

Group 1 – early flowering in winter and spring on the previous year's growth and can be pruned or just tidied up by removing old or damaged stems after flowering.

Group 2 – large-flowered hybrids with show-stopping blooms in spring and summer that also grow on the previous year's growth. These need to be pruned in February or March, reducing the growth by a third to ensure a good display. Cut away weak, damaged growth and cut stems to just above the strongest buds. Pruning after the first flush will also encourage a second flowering.

Group 3 – the late-flowering clematis, such as viticella, produce flowers on the current season's growth and are pruned in February or March. You can propagate from cuttings in spring to late summer, by layering late winter to spring, or from collected seed and possibly create something new.

Troubleshooting

Ensure you buy good, healthy plants, with at least two to three basal stems. If you don't plant clematis at the correct depth the plant can get clematis wilt. Don't be tempted to plant a clematis to cover a dead tree as this can become a host to disease, such as honey fungus.

Non-flowering can be a problem with clematis; however, this can usually be rectified with the correct pruning approach.

There are a few diseases that are generally caused by not providing the right conditions, water-stress, wind damage, or poor, shallow soil. Pruning below slime flux symptoms, for example, should allow the plant to re-shoot.

Good companions

Clematis pair with all types of plants, whether cottage-style roses and perennials, annuals around their base, trees or shrubs. Roses are a classic companion, and select varieties that flower at the same time and ideally are pruned at the same time, too, as they will be intertwined.

Growing through trees is another picture-perfect vignette – whether an early-flowering montana against pink and white crab apple blossom, or a high summer jewel-toned choice against the foil of a deep evergreen.

USEFUL SOURCES

RAYMOND EVISON CLEMATIS – 60 years breeding and developing clematis, sold on the website and available in garden centres worldwide (raymondevisonclematis.com)
TAYLOR CLEMATIS NURSERY – over 400 varieties and multiple RHS Gold Medalists (taylorsclematis.co.uk)
TYNINGS PLANTS – specialises in climbers, including clematis and honeysuckle (tyningsplants.co.uk)
HAYLOFT PLANTS – online plant nursery, specialising in rare, unusual and exciting plants (hayloft.co.uk)

Below: Clematis are superb on arches with their pliable stems. You can plant one or two on each side, and the best varieties to use are the vigorous and taller cultivars

All entwined

RECOMMENDED VARIETIES

Clematis 'Niobe' – Deep claret flowers early spring to autumn; pruning group two

Clematis 'Haku-Okan' – Striking large purple flowers through summer; pruning group two

Clematis 'Florida Sieboldii' – Abundant flowers followed by fluffy seedheads; pruning group three

Clematis Diamantina – Repeat-flowering double, each flower lasts up to four weeks; pruning group two

Clematis 'Ooh La La' – Compact, free-flowering variety, grows well in shade; pruning group three

Clematis 'Rhapsody' F. Watkinson – Light perfume, purple colour intensifies as it ages; pruning group two

Clematis Dancing King ('Zodaki') – Lilac flowers late spring to autumn, compact habit; pruning group two

Clematis Vickl – Compact, ideal for smaller gardens, Boulevard collection; pruning group three

Clematis Diana's Delight – Ideal for containers, repeat-flowering; pruning group two

English Cottage Gardens Handbook

YOUR GUIDE TO
Perfect pergolas

An easy choice for bringing privacy and romance to your garden, here's how to train a climber over a pergola

Words Teresa Conway

Create an impressive focal point and help define an area in your cottage garden with a pretty pergola. But first, it's important to consider size. If your pergola is too small it will feel claustrophobic; too large and it might dominate your space. Consider what you want to do under the pergola and make sure you have enough space to do it. Measure any outdoor furniture you are planning to place within the structure and ensure that you allow enough room for people to move around comfortably.

Choose the position
The best place for a pergola will depend on the layout of your garden and your reasons for including it in your design. Garden designer Katrina Kieffer-Wells (earthdesigns.co.uk) thinks pergolas work well in both sunny and shady spots depending on what time of day you will use it the most. 'If you have a south-facing garden a partially enclosed pergola can create a tranquil retreat and offer respite on a hot summer's day,' she says. 'In shady gardens, they can make a cosy night-time feature with the addition of ambient lights and hanging drapes.'

Planning permission
It's advisable to check local planning regulations before installing your pergola. Be sure to keep the total height from ground level around your house and neighbouring buildings to a maximum of 2.4m and consider what impact it could have on your neighbours.

Is it likely that it will block their view, for example? Katrina advises, 'If you are planning on adding decorative screens or a shade sail/canopy, think about how this could affect the amount or quality of light around it. Every situation is different so it's a good idea to check with your local authority and discuss your plans with your neighbours in advance.'

Preparing the site
First check to ensure there are no pipes, cables or hidden surprises underground where the upright posts are to be located. The footings of the pergola posts will have to be dug deep enough to ensure the pergola does not move or rock in the wind. 'It is worth checking the site by putting up some bamboo garden stakes first,' says garden designer

Left: Secluded seating area designed by Rebecca Smith (rsgardendesign.co.uk)
Above: The Round Pergola (by Agriframes) is perfect for creating a magical walkway filled with roses or clematis

Perfect pergolas

Rebecca Smith (rsgardendesign.co.uk). 'Will the pergola block a nice view from an upstairs room or will it help to hide an eyesore? It is much better to play around with the site before committing to the build to ensure the pergola is in the best place in your garden.' If you aren't confident in installing a sound structure yourself then seek the help of a local tradesperson.

Top right:
Go for a more rustic look with a log frame

We love...

'Repeat flowering roses combine well with honeysuckle for a scented haven in the summer. For winter interest, try clematis cirrhosa Wisley Cream or Freckles, which bloom from December to March, so the flowers can be appreciated at face level,' recommends Rebecca Smith.

Planting advice
Choose the right plants to cover your structure

A pergola is the ideal way to introduce real drama and, with the right planting, it can transform a walkway or seating area. Planting also helps to blend the structure naturally into your garden. Andrew Downey, Agriframes managing director, advises to 'start by planning the basic shape you want as soon as you plant your climber – flowers are produced more abundantly on horizontal stems rather than vertical ones, so tie stems along the cross bars of your pergola as soon as you can and keep tying them throughout the season to create a really good framework. Don't forget to bring stems to the inside of the frame as well as to cover it so that you can enjoy flowers and fragrance as you walk underneath.'

Clematis cirrhosa Wisley Cream will give you white blooms in winter

English Cottage Gardens Handbook 33

Forever green

Forming the structural backbone of the cottage garden, evergreens, with their foliage in shades of greys, golds, reds, silver and variegated forms, should not be overlooked for the potential they offer

Words Teresa Conway

Whether creating a towering hedge, an archway into a secret garden, or providing year-round interest in beds or containers, evergreens allow us to protect and divide areas as well as acting as a foil to ephemeral infill. They can provide impact, be used as specimens in containers or landscaping, as punctuation points and visual breaks in borders, or be clipped into fanciful topiary.

There are hundreds of varieties of evergreens, from dwarf to towering shrubs and trees, an array of flowering perennials and climbers, along with quiet little groundcovers, many of which are low-maintenance. Providing variety and versatility to enjoy throughout the year, an evergreen palette creates long-term interest.

Looking to the past

All through garden history evergreens have been relied on to create elegant gardens of lasting beauty. The clipping and moulding of plant shapes has a long tradition in both the East and West. Hedges and geometric shapes of topiary in Roman and Renaissance gardens gave them form, while wander through a classical Italian garden, with few flowers but manicured geometric forms and hedges delineating the space and the emphasis on symmetry and proportion, and you can't fail to be inspired. Formal French gardens made expert use of elaborate box parterres, rows of high clipped hedges and fine topiary for ordered perfection, while in Elizabethan knot gardens, hedges lent definition and sophistication to simple plantings of lavender, rosemary and cottage plants.

Defining boundaries

Hedging is an invaluable element to create privacy, divide space, provide wind protection for more tender plants or be a transition from formal to informal areas. As well as the classic evergreen tightly clipped hedging of plants such as yew, holly and box, a more informal softer hedging of mixed evergreen shrubs, such as glossy camellias, hebe, rambling roses or low-growing santolina and lavender, may suit your garden. Spiky grasses and tuft-forming plants, including carex or *Ophiopogon planiscapus* 'Nigrescens', can also look attractive as informal low borders to a space.

Think about the growth rate of the plant and what is manageable for you so that your hedging choice doesn't get out of hand. To add visual depth, fringe hedges with other plants, such as dark green box with a ribbon of low-growing silver-foliaged *Stachys byzantina*, lamb's ear, or the lime green froth of semi-evergreen *Alchemilla mollis*.

Planting ideas

In autumn and winter evergreens add reliable

Left: Clipping 'windows' into evergreen hedges can provide tempting glimpses of garden areas beyond, as here, where the opening frames the view of a small wildflower meadow, while ribbons of lavender and allium fringe the boundary
Above: Clipping evergreens gives year-round structure, especially in a formal garden. Infill with seasonal highlights, such as spires of alliums and cascading wisteria

consistency of texture and contrast to beds and borders as herbaceous perennials die back. These year-round performers include an array of flowering hardy perennials, ornamental grasses and climbers, which can be mixed into existing beds, or used to create container displays.

Evergreens with variegated foliage are very versatile. Some are subtle, in combinations of green and white, ideal to light up a dark corner; others are showy with technicolour gold, orange, red and pink pigmentation as accents that pop out against dark-green foliage.

Variegated foliage can also be used to pick out the colours of accompanying flowers, to harmonise or form complementary contrasts. Some evergreen foliage changes hues through the seasons, such as abelia, which intensifies from lime green to dark green; nandina goes from tints of red or purple to intense bright red in autumn; or trailing euonymus that turns dark purple in winter, providing interest among a uniform palette.

Add highlights with flowering evergreens and those that have autumn and winter berries, their vibrant jewels a visual delight as well as providing a valuable and reliable food source for visiting birds to forage.

Evergreen climbers and wall-climbing shrubs are particularly useful in small gardens to cover walls, fences or pergolas. To avoid looking too similar in a swathe of green, choose evergreens with different-sized foliage, some with added splashes of colour from berries and flowers, or others with silver or variegated leaves.

Topiary accents are also a classic choice for visual punctuation through beds and borders and can be made with a variety of plants. Choose shrubs with an attractive form that won't overpower, cut out the light or take nutrients from existing plants.

An architectural presence

Architectural evergreens become year-round living sculptures, acting as focal points or planted in groups for stunning massed displays. ➤

Above: Holly is a versatile evergreen, ideal for clipping into topiary or using in mixed hedging, with the added bonus of the jewel-like berries. The variegated foliage of 'Ripley Gold' adds another element

'Good husbandry is important; plants sometimes need a haircut and a makeover,' advises Angus White, founder and former owner of Architectural Plants nursery in Sussex (www.architecturalplants.com). 'The true creativity begins about three years after the planting is complete. Clipping, shaping and manicuring of evergreens ensures that, come winter, they are looking shapely and beautiful. Knowing what to remove, what to shape and how to meld your beloved collection of plants into a gigantic piece of delicious sculpture, is important,' adds Angus.

Now owned by Guy White, Architectural Plants specialises in evergreens such as European and Japanese topiary, including cloud-pruned *Ilex crenata* or Japanese holly, hardy palms, bamboos, plants for screening and many rare evergreen trees.

In winter, evergreens come to the forefront while other plants in the garden slumber, bringing interest to beds and borders, and presenting a glistening framework in early morning frost.

Above: For drought-tolerant choices, use repeated domes of tough and reliable hebe and lavender. Trimming them prevents the plants getting woody and ensures better flowering

Bottom right: Standard lollipops of Photinia 'Red Robin' make a striking statement and are echoed in the burgundy foliage colours of bergenias and heucheras

Some of the best evergreens

HEDGES – yew, holly, ceanothus, laurel, germander, box, griselinia, pittosporum, photinia, berberis, camellia, privet, grevillea, cotoneaster, *Viburnum tinus*, *Phillyrea latifolia*, *Lonicera nitida*

TOPIARY – yew, box, ilex, bay, ivy, privet, laurel, osmanthus, *Phillyrea latifolia*

POTS – dwarf conifers, phormium, cordyline, yucca, calamagrostis, panicum, ivy, box, skimmia, coprosma, camellia, gaultheria, heuchera

CLIMBERS – akebia, lonicera, *Trachelospermum jasminoides* or star jasmine, *Clematis armandii*, *Hydrangea seemannii*, *Hedera helix*, passionflower, pyracantha, solanum

BORDERS – azalea, bay, camellia, ceanothus, choisya, heather, hebe, lavender, santolina, rosemary, pittosporum, erysimum, pieris, dwarf conifers, box

GROUNDCOVERS AND ROCKERIES – ajuga, arabis, aubrieta, bergenia, carex, erica, festuca, iberis, liriope, ophiopogon, saxifrage, thyme, vinca, *Viburnum davidii*

SHADE – ajuga, asplenium, aucuba, bergenia,

Forever green

Cloud-pruning Ilex crenata trees echoes the artistry of Japan and these slow-growing, densely foliaged plants do well in sun or part shade

choisya, euonymus, hedera, epimedium, liriope, podocarpus, skimmia
SUN – lavender, santolina, erysimum, conifers, cistus, pittosporum, photinia, lavatera, grevillea, cordyline, ceanothus, phormium, rosemary, phlomis, myrtus, *Fremontodendron* 'California', leptospermum, callistemon, eryngium, thrift, cistus, armeria, erigeron
VARIEGATED – elaeagnus, euonymus, agave, aucuba, osmanthus, pittosporum, ligustrum, phormium, ilex, lamium, hebe, photinia, coprosma, pieris, abelia, yucca, cordyline, daphne, hedera
SILVER – eryngium, lavender, pittosporum, santolina, curry plant, artemisia, convolvulus, senecio, melianthus, perovskia, teucrium
BERRIES – holly, berberis, cotoneaster, arbutus, nandina, pyracantha, skimmia, yew, gaultheria, hypericum
SCENTED FLOWERS – choisya, daphne, muraya, osmanthus, sarcococca, *Trachelospermum jasminoides*, *Magnolia grandiflora*
ARCHITECTURAL – cordyline, euphorbia, festuca, itea, *Magnolia grandiflora*, phormium, stipa, yucca, bamboo, palms, succulents ●

YOUR GUIDE TO
Making the cut

Learn how to take plant cuttings, and fill your pots and borders
with an unlimited supply of your favourite varieties

Words Melanie Griffiths

Not only is taking plant cuttings one of the most frugal and sustainable garden ideas, but it is also one of the most enjoyable. There is no greater pleasure than nurturing new plants and watching them grow large enough to take pride of place in your cottage garden.

Growing plants from cuttings will allow you to recreate the specific variety, and is suitable for a huge number of plants, including most shrubs, hardy and tender perennials, hedging plants, climbers, certain trees and fruits, and many perennial herbs.

'Taking cuttings from plants, or propagating as it is technically called, is easy once you know how,' says plantswoman Sarah Raven. 'We take cuttings each year to give us plants for next spring and as insurance in case we need to replace any frost-killed plants.'

When to make the cut

It's important to determine the right stage to take cuttings from your plant.

Softwood cuttings are taken from fresh growth in the spring or early summer, when the stems are fairly soft and flexible. This method works best with plants that produce lots of new growth in the spring. Softwood cuttings are quick to root, however they are the most delicate type.

Semi-ripe cuttings are taken from plants in late summer or early autumn, once the current year's growth has had more time to become established. The method works well with almost any type of shrub, and has a high success rate. The cuttings may take root in the autumn, otherwise they will develop in the spring.

Hardwood cuttings are taken from the current year's growth, which has had a chance to mature into a strong 'woody' stem. Late autumn into winter is the ideal time. Hardwood cuttings are slow to root, but have a high success rate. It's a great method for many shrubs, fruits and trees.

Get the best growth

Select healthy growth from a non-flowering stem. With softwood and semi-ripe cuttings, look for the most vigorous growth, favouring stems that aren't too soft.

If taking hardwood cuttings, then you want growth from this year that has had time to mature. 'Ideally you are looking for material the thickness of a pencil,' says Charlene Chick-Seward, propagator at the National Trust's Nymans in West Sussex.

How to take cuttings

Ideally take plant cuttings in the morning, when the plant is full of water. 'With a sharp knife, take a short piece of stem from the plant,' says Sarah. 'Trim to just below a leaf joint, so the cutting is

5-6cm (2 inches) long.' To prepare your cuttings for planting, strip off all the leaves, leaving only the top pair.

'If the top pair of leaves are large, cut these in half across-ways,' explains Sarah. 'This seems brutal, but they will place less demand on the stem to draw up water. This makes the cutting more likely to root.'

Next, remove the stem tip. 'The growth hormone concentrates at the top, so by pinching it out, there's nowhere for it to go but down,' adds Sarah.

For hardwood cuttings, make a diagonal cut at the top, above a node. 'Make sure your top cut is on a slant to help avoid the top of the cutting rotting over winter,' says Charlene.

Plant cuttings in moist, free-draining compost. Charlene suggests a 50:50 mix of peat-free propagation compost and coarse grit.

Many gardeners like to first dip their cuttings into hormone rooting powder, but this is not necessarily essential.

'Insert your cuttings, well spaced, around the edge of the pots, about 5cm (2 inches) apart,' says Sarah. 'Placing them around the edge encourages quicker root formation as the new roots hit the side of the pot, break, and then branch into more lateral rootlets.'

If using long pots, plant the cuttings in a row. 'We place 8-10 cuttings in a long pot – but a small trench in the ground will also do,' adds Charlene.

Push the cuttings into compost, leaving each with at least one node below ground and above. Water.

Protect your cuttings

How much protection your cuttings require will depend on how tender they are.

'For softwood cuttings, cover the pot with a plastic bag supported on small canes to enclose moisture,' says Sarah. 'Pelargoniums are the exception of the tender perennials and don't need covering, but most things benefit from enclosure. If you have one, put them in a propagator with a bit of basal heat.'

Hardwood cuttings don't need much protection, but you should make sure the potting mix doesn't dry out. 'Hardwood cuttings do best outside in a sheltered position,' says Charlene.

'In the summer, keep your cuttings moist, and by late summer into early autumn, you can pot them on.'

Cuttings need good light but not direct sun.

How long does it take?

'Plant cuttings should root within two to three weeks,' says Sarah. 'You'll know they have taken when you see new growth at their tips. If it's before October, pot them on. Water only when the compost is dry.' Bear in mind that hardwood cuttings will take a lot longer to root, but all cuttings should be ready to plant out in the spring.●

Above: Propagating plants can be a great way to ensure you have replacements in case any of your plants are killed by an unexpected frost or pests

Lavender

Purple reign

With its aromatic properties and pollinator-friendly flowers, lavender makes a wonderful addition to any area of the garden

Words and **photographs** Leigh Clapp

Purple reign

Lavender is one of the most recognisable and popular plants, enjoyed for its refreshing fragrance and lovely coloured flowers. This versatile herb is easy to grow, has both medicinal and culinary uses and is attractive to pollinators – especially bees. There are many varieties from which to choose, so it is no wonder that this evergreen shrub has graced our garden beds and pots for centuries.

There are many different species and subspecies in the lavender family. However, the three main types that are grown, and which have different blooming seasons from spring to late-summer, are: *Lavandula angustifolia*, English lavender; *Lavandula stoechas*, French or Spanish lavender; and *Lavandula x intermedia*, lavandin.

The most widely recognised is English lavender, with its hardy, long-lived, neat plants and profusion of blooms in June or July, with stalwarts such as 'Hidcote' and 'Munstead'. *Stoechas* varieties are less hardy and shorter-lived, characterised by their distinctive sterile bracts, resembling two little stand-up ears. Flowering can be as early as May, with another flush in June, and a further late summer to autumn. Lavandin is a robust hybrid cross between *angustifolia* and *latifolia*, with tall mounds of grey foliage and long loose spikes of flowers in July or August.

When to plant

You can plant lavender any time between spring and autumn; however, planting in April or May is ideal, as the soil will be warming up and it will give your lavender time to establish through a full growing season. Many fresh plants will also be available at this time in your local garden centre or specialist nursery. Tender varieties are recommended to be planted from March to May.

Versatile varieties

'Lavenders simultaneously lend themselves to both formality and naturalness. There is nothing quite like a garden path bordered with just one variety of lavender. Equally a broad border with a mixture of lavenders of differing hues of blues, purples, pinks and whites, habits and flowering times can be an intoxicatingly beautiful blend,' says Simon Charlesworth, owner and master grower of Downderry Lavender.

Take into account the subtle colour differences available, level of hardiness and mature size. 'Use different species and cultivars for a longer display. For example, *Lavandula angustifolia* flowers earlier than *Lavandula x intermedia*, and by using cultivars of each species you can extend the flowering period,' explains RHS Wisley horticulturalist Toni Brown.

'We've used a mix of lavender species throughout the drought-tolerant Howard's Field Grass Garden at Wisley to extend the flowering season. Half-hardy lavenders, and in particular tender lavenders, offer striking foliage and unique flower spikes. These are well worth the extra time and effort,' she continues.

Where to grow

As a Mediterranean plant, lavender loves heat so plant it in full sun in free-draining, poor, dry or moderately fertile, chalky, neutral to alkaline soils. Half-hardy and tender lavenders need a sheltered spot. *Stoechas* and *x intermedia* however can grow in slightly acidic soils.

Mix in grit to heavy soils when planting to improve drainage and plant on a slight mound. They cope well with drought conditions and, in winter, wet soil rather than frost is more likely to kill half-hardy and frost-hardy lavenders.

'They will usually tolerate shade for a few hours a day, but lavenders require sharp drainage, so a sandy loam or lighter soil is ideal,' says Simon. 'Their natural habitat, akin to well-drained builders' rubble, is the scrubland environment of the hills of Southern France. Replicating this poor soil with its pH of 7-9 would be best.'

How to grow

Growing lavender is very easy, assuming the soil and site are optimised for them. Plants are usually sold in containers ready for planting, or as plug plants from some mail-order suppliers, which will need to be looked after for several months until large enough to be planted out.

Plant your container-bought lavender as soon as possible after purchasing, and to the same depth. Add some bonemeal in the planting hole ➤

Left: Choosing a mix of lavender colours and types is a charming idea for edging a path. It is also a great partner for a working beehive as the bright colours and rich scent make it easier for the foraging bees to spot
Above: Mix with olives and terracotta for a Mediterranean-inspired vibe

English Cottage Gardens Handbook 41

to help rooting out, firm down and water in, but avoid over watering.

'Space plants 45-90cm apart for informal planting, in groups of three,' recommends Simon. For hedging, space plants around 30cm apart. Be attentive in the first few weeks after planting if the weather is dry.

'Smaller plants in their first season should be trimmed below the first buds when they appear to encourage side shooting. Thereafter prune once the flowers have faded to ensure regrowth before the autumn. No further feeding is required and in fact is usually detrimental, leading to soft sappy growth and a floppy habit,' Simon advises. To propagate, take semi-ripe cuttings in late summer.

'Lavenders are drought-tolerant plants but water at the soil level to establish planting and encourage a good root system, though no overhead watering, as it damages the foliage,' adds Toni.

Growing in containers

Tender and half-hardy, as well as dwarf varieties, are ideal for a moveable summer display on the terrace – especially in terracotta pots. Place them in a sunny spot, away from overhanging trees. Containers need to be 30-40cm in diameter. 'Use a mix of one third each of soilless compost, John Innes No.2 or 3 and coarse grit. For feeding, add in a plug or two of slow-release fertiliser, which should last all season. Short plants are great for growing in pots, but watch out for the fibrous roots of all *stoechas* species and cultivars,' recommends Simon.

Water at regular intervals when the compost is drying out as they need more irrigation to develop a good root system, and re-pot regularly as they grow. Move containers of more tender varieties to shelter over winter.

How to care for lavender

Once established, lavenders are best left alone to be enjoyed, apart from their critical annual prune. 'Lavenders that flower from June to July should be pruned by mid-August, and those that flower July to August are best pruned by early September,' advises Simon.

Prune plants by about a third into the foliage to maintain their attractive domed habit when in flower. 'Stems at this level are about drinking straw thickness and regenerate well if there are plenty of small nodules or shoots below the cut,' adds Simon. 'By the time they go dormant in the autumn the lavenders should have re-clothed themselves with fresh young shoots that will harden off before the vagaries of the winter weather.'

Avoid cutting into hardwood where new shoots aren't present. You can also deadhead spent blooms to encourage further flowering. However, at the end of the flowering season, be sure to leave the seedheads to provide food for birds.

Trouble-shooting

Plants can develop a woody structure if not regularly clipped. 'Clipping harder can extend the plant's ornamental longevity, but avoid cutting hardwood where you can no longer see shoots, as then you risk losing the plant entirely,' says Toni.

Even if you have pruned your lavender regularly, older plants can get straggly and woody, so it is best to replace them. Other problems include root rot, if the plant is grown in wet or heavy soil. If these are the natural conditions in your garden, grow lavender in containers or raised beds. Always check the plant label to see how hardy the plant is, as only hardy varieties will survive winter outside.

Good companions

Lavenders get on well with other sun-loving flowers and herbs that thrive in the same conditions. Some of the most popular pairings include echinacea, roses, achillea, santolina, artemisia, sedums, daisies, zinnias and rosemary.

'We favour companion plants that are drought tolerant and can grow independently once established, as this enables a sustainable water management scheme and favours those adapted to a warmer climate. Plants that self-seed can be cost and time effective, too,' says Toni. 'We aim to select companion plants that provide extended interest but also provide for wildlife – simple flower forms favoured by pollinators.' At Wisley this includes scabious, cosmos, nepeta, eryngium, Californian poppies, agastache, salvias, perovskia, *Verbena bonariensis* and grasses.

LAVENDER SOURCES AND INSPIRATION
DOWNDERRY LAVENDER, Hadlow, Kent TN11 9SW. Home to the world's only Scientific National Plant Collection of lavender. Tel: 01732 810081; downderry-nursery.co.uk
RHS WISLEY, Surrey GU23 6QB. Lavender in drought-tolerant garden at Howard's Field, mass planted in front of Stone Pine Café and ribbons of lavender and rosemary on a viewing mound. Tel: 01483 224234; rhs.org.uk
LAVENDER WORLD. York-based family business selling a wide range of plants online. Tel: 01653 648008; lavenderworld.co.uk
MAYFIELD LAVENDER FARM, Banstead SM7 3JA. 25-acre organic lavender farm with café and shop. Open from 1 June. mayfieldlavender.com ●

Below: This sinuous, serpentine design by Alison Wear uses *Lavandula x intermedia* 'Grosso', the classic French lavender with low-growing lime green *Sesleria* 'Greenlee Hybrid', moor grass

Purple reign

RECOMMENDED VARIETIES

Lavandula angustifolia 'Hidcote' – Highly popular, compact, dense, fragrant deep violet flowers

Lavandula angustifolia 'Purple Treasure' – Compact shrub with grey-green foliage and ultraviolet flowers

Lavandula angustifolia 'Imperial Gem' – Silvery-green leaves and deep purple flowers

Lavandula x intermedia 'Grosso' – Vigorous, one of the strongest fragrances

Lavandula stoechas 'Pink Panache' – New, flamboyant variety with vibrant magenta pink ears

Lavandula angustifolia 'Miss Katherine' – The best of the pinks, highly fragrant blooms

Lavandula x intermedia 'Heavenly Angel' – Robust, aromatic leaves, with white flowers

Lavandula x intermedia 'Sussex' – Bushy evergreen shrub with the longest flowers of any hardy lavender

Lavandula stoechas 'Regal Splendour' – Aromatic leaves with enchanting velvet-purple flowers

English Cottage Gardens Handbook

Foxgloves

The perfect fit

Foxgloves are cottage garden favourites and make an eye-catching addition to any border with their tall, tubular blooms – find out how to get the best out of them

Words and **photographs** Leigh Clapp

Evoking old-fashioned storybook charm, foxgloves are at home in woodlands, hedgerows and cottage gardens. Their late spring or early summer appearance is appreciated for the naturalistic impact they bring, adding height and forming self-perpetuating colonies.

'There is a foxglove for almost any part of your garden, from the woodland shade to the hot sunny border,' explains Mary Baker, who, with husband Terry, holds the national collection of digitalis at their Botanic Nursery and Gardens in Wiltshire.

'Foxgloves give that height required early in the season in the cottage garden or mixed border,' explains Rosy Hardy of Hardy's Cottage Garden Plants in Hampshire.

Varieties of foxgloves

You are sure to know our pink, white or apricot varieties of native *Digitalis purpurea*, which self-seed extensively, their spires of bell flowers swaying in the breeze popping up sometimes a bit too promiscuously in our gardens. However, with 24 species of foxgloves, around 40 cultivars, and a geographic range through central and southern Europe, there are more varieties to try than you may realise, with a host of different colours, shapes and sizes to choose from.

'Over the years, breeding has brought in some new varieties that flower for a longer period with stronger colours,' explains Rosy Hardy. These easy-to-grow tubular blooms are a valuable source of pollen and are especially attractive to long-tongued bees. With a range of colours, from pinks and whites to apricots and yellows, drifts of foxgloves grace a wildlife-friendly garden.

Some foxgloves are hardy biennials, such as our two natives – *purpurea* and *albiflora* – which produce foliage and root growth in their first year, then flowering and setting seed in the next, before dying back. As they self-seed so freely, they can be thought of as short-lived perennials. Species foxgloves, on the other hand, are perennials, flower in July, and will last for three to five years.

'Foxgloves are misunderstood as most gardeners think they are biennials. The species come true from seed while the biennials cross-pollinate. Because of their ability to set seed easily, breeders can create wonderful hybrids that flower in their first year and continue to do so for a couple more years. Many set seed, but seldom recreate the parent they came from,' explains Mary Baker.

When to plant

Plant foxgloves in spring when the soil is warm and moist, to encourage root growth. There is a greater choice of seed varieties through mail-order specialists. Seeds are best sown between January and May. Seed collected from the pods can be sown straight away, or kept in a cool dry place and sown in a tray to grow on and then plant out in spring.

You can also grow from plug plants and garden-ready plants that will flower in the first year. The RHS doesn't recommend autumn planting for young plug plants; instead keep them in their pots in a sheltered spot over winter and then plant out in spring. Foxgloves are poisonous to the touch so always wear gloves when handling plants or seeds.

Where to grow

Foxgloves are one of the key plants of any woodland ➤

44 English Cottage Gardens Handbook

The perfect fit

The pastel apricot shades of the 'Sutton's Apricot' foxglove have such a soft, romantic hue that works charmingly with white and silver combinations, as here with the first cosmos and cynara foliage

English Cottage Gardens Handbook 45

garden as they thrive in dappled shade under large trees and shrubs. However, there are some species that require full sun to do well, so you can find varieties to suit your chosen location. Whether planted in sun or shade, they will supply statuesque height to the back of borders, with their flower spikes growing from 30cm up to 2m or more.

'Grow them in a group for best impact. The seed needs light to germinate, so choosing the correct variety for the area is important,' says Mary Baker.

Foxgloves like good air circulation and not being overcrowded, and will grow in any well-drained, moist soil, rich in organic matter, although acidic soil with a pH under 6.0 is ideal. Avoid very dry or very wet soils. Taller foxgloves need protection from strong winds.

How to grow

Growing foxgloves from seed is the most economical choice. You can scatter seeds directly in your garden but as they are so tiny you may get better success sowing them indoors on good-quality seed compost. Cover with the seeds with a little compost or vermiculite to keep them in place, pop in a propagator or polythene bag on a sunny windowsill and then into pots to grow on.

To get native foxgloves to self-seed around the garden, plant them two years in a row. For plug plants, pot on into individual pots, keep in a cool, frost-free spot, let them acclimatise and double in size then plant into the garden. Garden-ready plants are a bit larger and can be planted into pots to grow a little more or be planted straight into their garden position. Dig in some well-rotted compost before planting and then mulch over the surface. Space young plants 30-35cm apart so they can spread out their rosette of leaves.

'Modern F1 hybrids can typically be recognised by the flowers produced all around the stem; these sorts usually flower for 2-3 years but their seed is rarely good. Some herbaceous varieties, such as *Digitalis grandiflora* and *lutea*, can be divided. On the other hand, species foxgloves all come true from seed,' explains Mary Baker.

Container growing

Most foxgloves can be grown in large containers and there are also dwarf varieties available.

'When growing foxgloves in containers, be sure to use a quality compost and ensure that you feed the plant regularly; you can do this either with a slow-release fertiliser or liquid feed. Do not let the plant get pot bound and do not overwater them. Cutting back the spent flower stems encourages even more flower stems to grow,' says Mary Baker.

A mature foxglove can reach up to 5 metres in height, so you will need a large container.

'If you are planting foxgloves with other plants, make sure not to overcrowd them, as this could cause diseases like leaf spot. Foxgloves love humus-rich soil so add some of the most decomposed matter from your compost bin to the potting material. Tall foxgloves may also need support to stop them being damaged by winds. Place your container in an area of the garden that is in full sun or part shade,' says Adam Alexander, RHS horticulturalist at Wisley.

How to care for foxgloves

'With the exception of a couple of rare species, foxgloves are hardy, so don't mollycoddle them,' continues Mary Baker. Water newly planted foxgloves for the first few months to help them spread their roots. Once they have established in their rich soil, they should only require watering in dry summer spells.

Deadhead some of the flowers to conserve the energy of the plant and improve longevity but leave some to set seed and create the next generation. Harvest some of the seed of your favourite biennial to increase your stock. To do this, cut the stem with the seed capsules, place in a large paper bag and, once dry, the seed will fall out and will be ready to pack and store.

Troubleshooting

Foxgloves are generally trouble-free and easy to care for, although you may need to protect young plants from slugs and snails. If leaves are affected by fungal spots or powdery mildew, remove the diseased leaves or spray with a suitable fungicide. Chlorosis, or leaf yellowing, is a sign of nutrient deficiency. Aphids can be an issue so try to keep a healthy garden with lots of natural predators.

Good planting companions

These lovely flowers make a pleasing foil for old-fashioned roses, are at home with spring-flowering shrubs in borders or woodland clearings, and are attractive combined with summer bulbs, irises, hesperis and aquilegia.

'Digitalis work well with alliums and geums to give a wonderful early summer display. The perennial forms are great for later in the season, some in shadier places mixing well with grasses and heleniums,' says Rosy Hardy.

'You can use foxgloves in many different styles of gardening. For a natural woodland-style planting in an area with dappled shade, I would combine them with *Campanula rotundifolia*, common harebell, and ferns such as *Polystichum polyblepharum*, Japanese tassel fern. For a sunnier spot of the garden, I recommend a spring cottage-style planting. Foxgloves combined with peonies, roses and salvia will give you a show of flowers from late spring to autumn,' says Adam Alexander.

WHERE TO BUY

THE BETH CHATTO GARDENS AND NURSERY, Colchester CO7 7DB – woodland and water gardens. Open daily. Entry £8.45. Tel: 01206 822007; bethchatto.co.uk
THE BOTANIC NURSERY & GARDENS, Atworth, Wiltshire SN12 8NU – home to national collection of digitalis, with seeds, plugs and plants available. Tel: 07850 328756; thebotanicnursery.co.uk
HARDY'S COTTAGE GARDEN PLANTS, Whitchurch, Hants RG28 7FA – Award-winning nursery specialising in herbaceous perennials.
Tel: 01256 896533; hardysplants.co.uk •

The perfect fit

RECOMMENDED VARIETIES

Digitalis ferruginea – Also known as rusty foxglove, flowers June to September

Digitalis x mertonensis – Also known as strawberry foxglove, perennial hybrid, flowers in late spring/early summer, strawberry shade

Digitalis purpurea 'Pam's Choice' – One of the best cultivars, features tall, strong spires

Digitalis 'Goldcrest' – Perennial, peachy-yellow, summer to autumn

Digitalis 'Foxlight Ruby Glow' – Hybrid, summer long blooms, grows best in light shade

Digitalis purpurea – Quintessential native foxglove, summer flowering, biennial

Digiplexis 'Falcon Fire' – Cross native and Canary Island foxglove, long flowering period

Digitalis purpurea f. albiflora – White-flowered foxglove, flowers June to July, favourite of Gertrude Jekyll

Digitalis purpurea 'Sugar Plum' – Sturdy perennial, purple-white flowers from May to July

English Cottage Gardens Handbook 47

Design YOUR Perfect BORDER

Garden designer Tabi Jackson Gee lays out six border styles that you can plant now to reap the benefits next summer

It's so tempting to go to the garden centre on a sunny day and buy a variety of plants that you like the look of, without any research on what they will work well with or where they will thrive in your outdoor space.

That's where garden designers come in. We think of gardens as a whole, creating areas that share a common visual language and planting schemes with different environments in mind.

Autumn is a great time to be planning your borders for next spring and summer. Not only are the bare root plants and trees available to buy now much less expensive, but you will be giving your new border plenty of time to get its roots in, at the same time as sowing seeds and planting bulbs for the new season.

Design your perfect border

LIGHT SHADE

Perhaps it's because we can't see it, but scent is often overlooked when it comes to garden design. However a garden without fragrance isn't fulfilling its potential. Your outdoor space should delight all your senses, and this border is created to have something flowering throughout the year that offers just that. Most of the plants I've chosen are fairly hardy, but the border will do best in a spot that has light shade for at least some of the day, and that doesn't get waterlogged.

Hyacinthus orientalis 'Delft Blue'

Osmanthus delavayi

Daphne 'Perfume Princess'

Lavandula angustifolia

The scented one

TOP TIPS

- *Daphne* 'Perfume Princess', like most daphnes, doesn't like its roots getting dry – so make sure you keep them well watered during the hotter months.
- Put your *Hyacinthus orientalis* 'Delft Blue' near a path so you can enjoy its amazing scent.
- Both the daphne and osmanthus will appreciate a good mulch once a year.
- Add the sweet peas (*Lathyrus odoratus*) into the border in the summer to complement the lavender in both colour and scent.
- Don't forget to cut some of these stems to enjoy indoors, too!

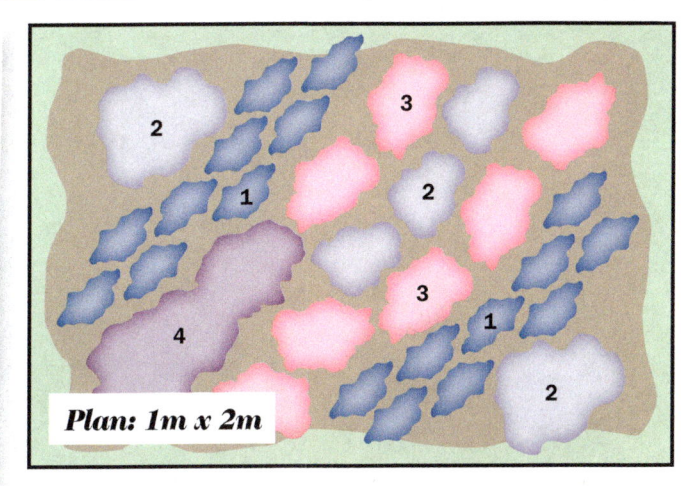

Optional extras

Lathyrus odoratus 'Oxford Blue'

Lathyrus odoratus 'Charlie's Angel'

Plan: 1m x 2m

- **1.** *Hyacinth orientalis* 'Delft Blue'
- **2.** *Daphne* 'Perfume Princess'
- **3.** *Lavandula angustifolia*
- **4.** *Osmanthus delavayi*

OPTIONAL EXTRAS *Lathyrus odoratus* 'Oxford Blue'; *Lathyrus odoratus* 'Charlie's Angel'

SHADY SPOTS

There are no two ways about it, shady gardens or shady areas can be a challenge. So much so that people often write them off as a sad corner, or use them for bicycle storage, bonfires or sheds. But there are many beautiful plants that enjoy shade, even some evergreen ones. I think this scheme would be very useful along a side return or a front drive where you want evergreens but also something to enjoy in terms of flowers and scent. The sarcococca's common name is sweet box and its smell is divine. It also shows up in the depths of winter when we often need cheering up the most.

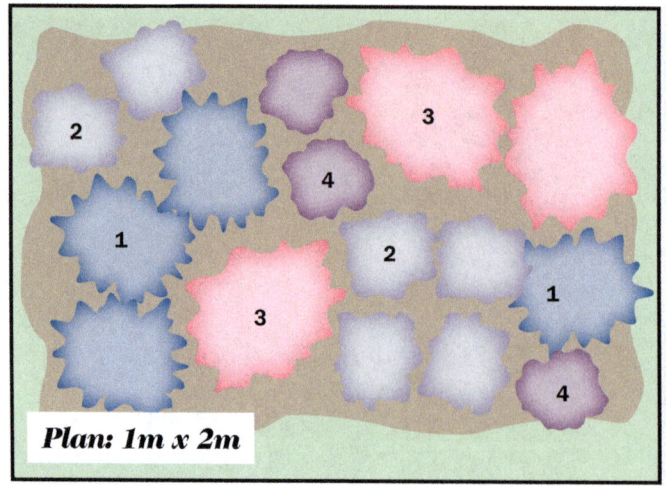

Plan: 1m x 2m

● **1.** Bergenia 'Ice Queen' ● **2.** Heuchera 'Black Beauty' ● **3.** Sarcococca hookeriana 'Winter Gem' ● **4.** Pachysandra terminalis
OPTIONAL EXTRAS Cyclamen hederifolium; Anemone blanda 'White Splendour'

Optional extras

Cyclamen hederifolium

The evergreen one

Bergenia 'Ice Queen'

Anemone blanda 'White Splendour'

Heuchera 'Black Beauty'

Sarcococca hookeriana 'Winter Gem'

Pachysandra terminalis

TOP TIPS

● Lightly prune the sarcococca to help keep its shape.
● Remove faded flower spikes from the heuchera, and watch out for vine weevil.
● After flowering, remove the flowerheads from the bergenia and apply a slow-release fertiliser around the plant. Lift and divide large clumps in early spring as these can get quite carried away.
● Place the sarcococca near a pathway so you can enjoy its wonderful scent in the winter.
● If you add the Anemone blanda, plant it under a tree or a shrub, where it will create a lovely carpet of white flowers in the spring.

Design your perfect border

SUNNY & DRY

Gravel gardens aren't just for the Mediterranean, as anyone who's visited Beth Chatto's 'car park' garden will know. Here, in this border, peachy oranges and zesty greens rustle together to create an ethereal scheme. This style of planting requires little watering; the gravel mulch helps the soil retain moisture and keeps weeds at bay. It is ideal for raised beds where you can enjoy the swaying grasses from indoors or out, but it will work in most sunny, dry spots and the plants will tolerate fairly poor soil quite happily.

TOP TIPS

- Give these plants space; this is not a crowded border but a lighter touch planting scheme that lets each species sing.
- Unlike bigger, tougher grasses, *Stipa tenuissima* doesn't need an annual chop; instead, pull your fingers through it gently to remove any dead parts.
- Deadhead the geum regularly in the summer to prolong flowering.
- Experiment with bulbs and seeds; try adding alliums or nerines for colour before and after summer.
- Choose a light, bright gravel for your mulch layer – it will make the colours in the border really pop.

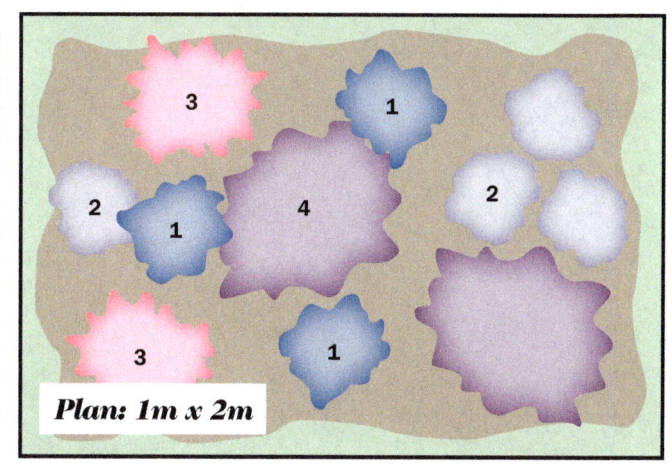

Geum 'Mai Tai'

Stipa tenuissima

Iris 'Alaska'

Euphorbia characias subsp. *wulfenii*

The gravel one

Optional extras

Papaver somniferum 'Lilac Pompom'

Achillea 'Peachy Seduction'

Plan: 1m x 2m

- **1.** *Stipa tenuissima* ● **2.** *Geum* 'Mai Tai' ● **3.** *Iris* 'Alaska'
- **4.** *Euphorbia characias* subsp. *wulfenii*

OPTIONAL EXTRAS *Papaver somniferum* 'Lilac Pompom'; *Achillea* 'Peachy Seduction'

FULL SUN

Inspired by the prairies of North America (parts of which have a similar climate to areas of the UK), prairie-style planting is increasingly popular due to its wonderful matrix of colours and textures – consisting of grasses and flowers that need the same conditions – and its natural, unmanicured look. Like wildflower meadows, these landscapes are loose and relaxed – there isn't any formal topiary in sight. Most of the plants chosen here are versatile and will work on clay and chalk soils, but will appreciate free-draining soil. A spot in full sun will give the best results.

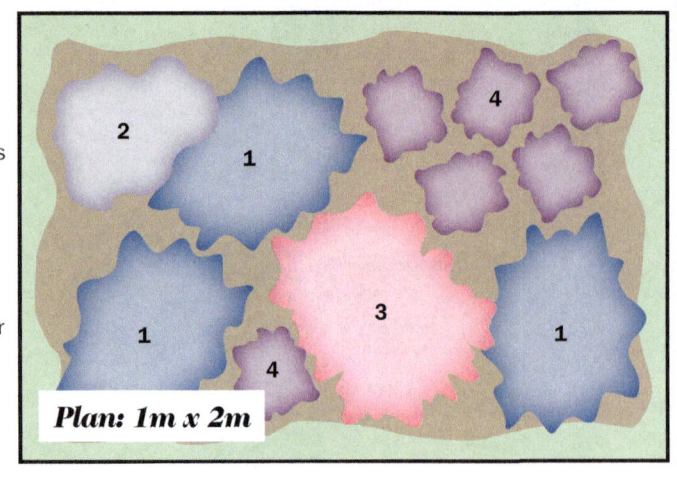

Plan: 1m x 2m

- **1.** *Sanguisorba* 'Tanna'
- **2.** *Carex testacea* 'Prairie Fire'
- **3.** *Molinia caerulea* subsp. *arundinacea* 'Transparent'
- **4.** *Echinacea purpurea* **OPTIONAL EXTRAS** *Papaver rhoeas* 'Amazing Grey'; *Allium cernuum*

Optional extras

Papaver rhoeas 'Amazing Grey'

Carex testacea 'Prairie Fire'

Allium cernuum

The wild one

Echinacea purpurea

Sanguisorba 'Tanna'

Molinia caerulea subsp. *arundinacea* 'Transparent'

TOP TIPS

- Give the molinia lots of space and keep an eye on it as it establishes so it doesn't get overshadowed by the other plants.
- You can just cut these plants back once a year in early spring; sanguisorba in particular looks beautiful through the winter thanks to its floaty seedheads.
- The poppies can be sown in the autumn and they'll surprise you by where they come up.
- Having said that, be careful not to be too diligent with your weeding – don't accidentally pull the poppies out!
- Repeat this scheme over a bigger scale for greater drama, mixing in dogwoods for structure and more winter colour.

52 English Cottage Gardens Handbook

Design your perfect border

PARTIAL SHADE

Colourful, wild, rambling, inviting… a cottage garden is quintessentially English. But while the variety of classic bulbs, annuals, perennials, flowering shrubs and climbers that we associate with it can be used in many settings, it's only when they're carefully combined that they create that romantic look. Plenty of light and sun will make this border easy to grow and care for. The plants I've chosen here will tolerate partial shade and most slightly acidic, slightly alkaline or neutral soils.

TOP TIPS

- This isn't a scheme for the faint-hearted with its mix of bold colours, but it's certainly cheery!
- Divide the geranium after a few years if it gets too big for its boots.
- Go big with the bulbs; most of the plants in this scheme flower in the summer – bulbs will reward you with fab spring colour.
- *Alcea rosea* 'Halo Blush' is a big hollyhock, so position it at the side of the border, especially if don't want to block a view.
- If you repeat this across a bigger space, add some rambling roses climbing up obelisks or a sunny south-facing wall.

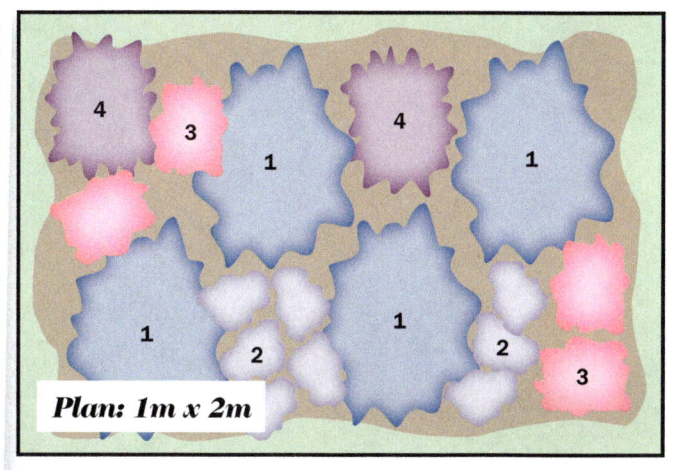

Thalictrum delavayi 'Hewitt's Double'

Alcea rosea 'Halo Blush'

Geranium 'Orion'

Tiarella 'Pink Skyrocket'

The classic one

Optional extras

Tulipa 'Peach Blossom'

Narcissus 'Ice King'

Plan: 1m x 2m

- **1.** *Thalictrum delavayi* 'Hewitt's Double' ● **2.** *Tiarella* 'Pink Skyrocket' ● **3.** *Geranium* 'Orion' ● **4.** *Alcea rosea* 'Halo Blush'
OPTIONAL EXTRAS *Tulipa* 'Peach Blossom'; *Narcissus* 'Ice King'

English Cottage Gardens Handbook 53

FULL SUN/ PARTIAL SHADE

Many of us want to have a low-maintenance garden, and there are many ways to achieve this. Usually evergreen shrubs are a good bet, as they do their thing with little help (except for the occasional pruning). But if you'd like a bit more interest, this border is a good start – and still very low-key in terms of care, thanks to its mix of shrubs, grasses and long-flowering perennials. This scheme would like full sun but will tolerate part shade. Just make sure the site is not too windy, or the hydrangea will get battered.

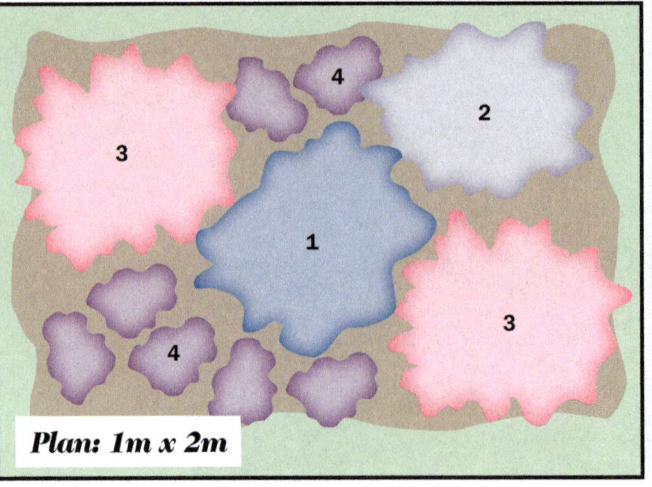

Plan: 1m x 2m

● **1.** *Pittosporum tobira* 'Nanum' ● **2.** *Hydrangea arborescens* Strong Annabelle ● **3.** *Miscanthus sinensis* ● **4.** *Geranium* Dreamland ('Bremdream') **OPTIONAL EXTRAS** *Tulipa* 'Lilac Perfection'; *Muscari* 'Baby's Breath'

Optional extras

Muscari 'Baby's Breath'

Tulipa 'Lilac Perfection'

Miscanthus sinensis

The easy one

Pittosporum tobira 'Nanum'

Geranium Dreamland ('Bremdream')

Hydrangea arborescens Strong Annabelle

TOP TIPS

● Give the miscanthus plenty of space and put it in a spot where it gets a good amount of sun.
● Leave the flowerheads on the hydrangea over winter; its golden colours will look fantastic against the tall, textural miscanthus.
● Keep the pittosporum's shape nice and rounded to contrast with the height and spread of the other plants.
● *Muscari* 'Baby's Breath' has a wonderful scent, so put it somewhere that you can enjoy it.
● If you like this planting scheme and want to try something a bit higher maintenance, this would work really well combined with the wild border in a larger space.

Save & sow

YOUR GUIDE TO save & sow

Learn how to harvest seeds from flowers and crops to increase your garden stock for free

Words Melanie Griffiths

Harvesting seeds from flowers and crops is a sustainable, frugal way to create an endless supply of your favourite varieties.

Many annual and biennial flowers will happily self-sow, too, so look out for familiar seedlings from the likes of foxgloves, poppies and cosmos popping up in beds the following year, as these can just be replanted in your preferred locations.

Bear in mind that not all plants will produce seeds that grow 'true to type' – meaning they won't be clones of the parent plant. This can be an issue in particular when growing crops, as it can affect flavour – so stick to species and heirloom varieties, and avoid saving seed from hybrids. However, many gardeners enjoy experimenting to see what varieties they can create.

Early autumn is the ideal time to start gathering seeds once the plants are over. 'Seeds are naturally packaged in a variety of pods, cones, berries, catkins, capsules, nuts, winged seed or exploding seed heads,' says *Period Living*'s resident gardening expert Leigh Clapp. 'Choose a dry day to collect ripened seeds from healthy plants, before the seed heads open and disperse their contents.

'Hang or place the seed heads on a warm windowsill or greenhouse bench to dry. If the pods or capsules don't open when dry, release the seeds by gently crushing them. For fruits and berries, mash them in a sieve, rinse away the pulp and leave the seeds to dry. You can place a bag over exploding seed heads and gently shake them out.'

Some of the easiest plants to grow from seed include alliums, nigella, poppies, cosmos, calendula, zinnias, cleome and sunflowers. Store your collected seeds in paper packets in a cool, dry place, ideally in a tin or container. Label each packet with the name of the plant and the date harvested. Some seeds can be sown immediately; most will be stored until spring.

Top plants to try

Sunflowers are one of the easiest flowers from which to harvest seeds. You can either save the seeds for growing, or harvest them for eating – in which case, choose a variety bred to produce large, edible seeds, like Russian Giant or Titan.

If harvesting sunflower seeds for eating, you may need to protect from birds by tying a paper bag over the blooms, or you can cut the stalks before they are ready and hang indoors to dry.

To harvest the seeds, firstly you need to remove the chaff (spent inner flowers and outer petals) – this may drop off on its own, or you might need to pick or rub it off. Mature sunflower seeds will come out of the flower easily when you firmly rub your fingers over them – place a bowl beneath to catch them as they drop. If the seeds don't fall out easily, allow a few more days to mature.

Rinse the harvested seeds in a colander and then pick out the debris to clean them. Place the seeds in a single layer on a paper towel to dry for a couple of days before storing in a packet.

Zinnias can be grown from seeds harvested from all varieties, however not all will grow true to type. 'Select varieties that have been open pollinated, as opposed to hybrids – which can vary widely in the next generation,' says Leigh. If you have a few different types of open-pollinated zinnias, they can become cross-pollinated. You can prevent this by planting different types far apart, or by covering the buds of one or two flowers with a paper or mesh bag before they open. This will prevent pollinators from getting in, but allow the flower to go to seed.

As the petals wither away, the seed begins to form where the centre of the flower was. This will gradually dry out. Once it has turned brown and feels dry to the touch, the seeds can be harvested. To do this, cut the seed head off the plant. Tap it onto a piece of paper and you'll see the individual seeds fall out. Pour the seed into a paper envelope.

Tomatoes can be grown well from seed, but only heirloom varieties – hybrids will not grow true to the parent. If the tomato is ripe, then the seeds are ready to harvest. If you have over-ripe tomatoes that you don't want to eat, harvesting their seeds is a great way to ensure they don't go to waste.

Harvesting tomato seeds is as simple as cutting open the tomato and scooping out the seeds. However, the seeds will be covered in a gelatinous liquid, so you need to clean and dry them before storing. This liquid can be difficult to remove, but it may prevent the seeds from germinating.

Scoop the seeds into a sieve and gently work them free from the liquid under running water. It's a good idea to soak the seeds for a day or two in water before rinsing them off, to make sure the film is removed. To save and store your tomato seeds to plant next year, you will need to dry them out so that they don't go mouldy. To do this, place them on a plate and let them sit out for 4-5 days until they're completely dry. Avoid using paper towel, as they will stick to it.

Patio delight

Extend your living space by creating the perfect patio for relaxing and entertaining, taking inspiration from cottage gardens for maximum period charm

Words Teresa Conway

Outdoor spaces should be seen as an extension of our homes, so whether you are augmenting an existing patio or adding one from scratch, it is important to create a design that complements your property. Consider how you would like to utilise the space, as well as how your ideas will work with the design of your home and garden. The perennially loved cottage garden style is a look that translates to almost any house era, so use this as a source of inspiration to add charm to your patio area.

Green living

Selecting patio paving can be a challenge, especially when you want to find a material that complements your house and garden, suits your budget and is also kind to the planet. 'To keep a patio soft in terms of its impact on the earth, think about which stones you use. Reclaimed and local will have the least impact and carbon footprint, while also adding rustic charm. Stone takes thousands of years to be created, and will last a long time, too,' says landscape architect Marian Boswall.

Mixed materials add interest and can be used to break up a large area; however, it is also important to think through the design carefully so it doesn't look too haphazard. Flat areas for seating could use flagstones, whereas pathways and surrounding borders could use various-sized stones, for example.

'When it comes to creating a sustainable patio, aim for materials that have been sourced or manufactured within Britain; Yorkstone, such as Scoutmoor, is strong and durable,' says Chris Griffiths, head of product sustainability at Marshalls. 'There are also UK-made concrete paving ranges that replicate the look and feel of imported natural stone.' Pavers can be made from recycled materials or can be reclaimed, both of which are highly sustainable with an aesthetic that is particularly well suited to a cottage style. 'Pay attention to drainage, too, especially if you live in an area at risk of flooding,' adds Chris.
'A permeable surface will sustainably deal with rainwater, and Driveline Drain is a drainage option that blends subtly into the paving, without compromising the overall look.' Permeable paving options include brick, stone, pavers and gravel.

Potted perfection

Containers offer the possibility of a moveable display that can highlight the seasons or even put you in a holiday mood. Whether an eclectic mix of pots or a carefully orchestrated scene, container planting allows you to express yourself in a way

Patio delight

Left: Aim to use reclaimed or locally made stone or gravel in your patio area **This image:** Arbours add charming shady nooks to a cottage garden

Pots can add charm to any outdoor space

that you can adapt, allowing you to change the look in an instant.

Seasonal annuals can be added to permanent evergreens, and you can echo the colours of the house for co-ordinated combinations, be harmonious with your palette, or go for bright, eclectic energy with your plant choices.

Growing up

Create an intimate, shady nook where you can sit and enjoy the views over your garden. Arbours are perfect for adding cottage charm. They can be rustic with reclaimed timbers or a metal arch disappearing under a topping of entwining vines and blooms. Think about whether you want shade year-round with evergreen climbers, such as star jasmine, climbing euonymus, potato vine and passionflower, or just for the heat of summer with deciduous options, from clematis to climbing roses.

For privacy, back the area with large-leafed variegated ivy or other evergreens and fringe with frothy perennials and colourful annuals.

Take shelter

In more exposed locations, a sunken patio lined by low walls still allows you to gaze over views, while protecting you from the wind.

Overleaf, this intimate space at Follers Manor in the Sussex Downs is formed by sinking the patio ➤

English Cottage Gardens Handbook 57

and lining it with low, flint walls. The design by Ian Kitson follows the contours of the surrounding borrowed landscape, with the serpentine walls echoed by sinuous planting. Simple clipped buxus hedging and repeated ribbons of crimson penstemon, drought-tolerant purple salvias, and accents from spires of phlomis accentuate the design.

Above: The sunken patio at Follers Manor in the Sussex Downs
Below: Add character to garden furniture with paint

Colour confidence

Brighten your patio with painted structures. Try colour psychology, such as orange and yellow to stimulate appetite, bright tones to boost the mood, or tranquil harmonious cool and calming tones for a space to relax in.

'Preparation is key when painting to ensure the longevity of outdoor structures and furniture. These things are likely to face all conditions throughout the year. For wooden items it is vital to fill cracks, holes and other imperfections using wood filler,' says Michael Rolland, MD of The Paint Shed.

Sand and prepare the surface and choose the right type of paint. 'Not checking the weather before painting is a common mistake. You may think that painting in full sun will speed up the process, but the faster the sun dries the paint, the more mistakes there will be, such as drag marks and dried drips. Overcast and warm is ideal,' adds Michael.

Salvaged style

Have fun finding interesting reclaimed pieces to use, from seating to decorative detailing. Scour local salvage yards or community websites. Dressing your outdoor area in a unique way with handcrafted or homemade upcycling will add individual personality to the space, while also saving items from going to landfill.

Timber offcuts or pallets could be reused for seating or to form a vertical garden, old crates can hold containers, and there are always lots of galvanized items, such as old coppers and troughs for use as characterful planters.

Hide away

Position a cottage patio in a secluded spot hidden away from the wider garden – a secret place for a meal, or to sit and enjoy your favourite novel

Patio delight

This image: Create a tranquil haven with chaotic plantings around the patio
Below: Local salvage yards may have some treasures you can reclaim to use in your garden.

with a cup of tea. Immerse yourself in a touch of wildness with self-sown flowers popping up, vines entwining supports, eclectic pots, and encircling shrubs, for a secret patio feel.

Plants such as *Alchemilla mollis*, erigeron and *Sisyrinchium striatum* will find their way into nooks and crannies. Wafting ornamental grasses and perennials are lovely enclosing the space to create your garden escape. A curved bed partway round the patio could form a living framework that divides the area.

Fresh taste

Edibles don't just belong on the veg plot. Incorporate them in your cottage patio design and enjoy their beauty as well as the ease of harvesting, for a seating or dining area with a difference.

Look for compact varieties of crops for containers, climbers for cane supports, and try low-growing edging with wild strawberries or ribbons of thyme to utilise the space creatively. 'Help yourself' takes on a whole new meaning with homegrown organic garnishes to hand.

Incorporate edibles into your patio space with pots

Peonies

Royal beauty

Long-lived and admired for their glamorous flowers, peonies offer timeless elegance to the garden

Words and **photographs** Leigh Clapp

The flush of voluptuous peonies each year may be short, but they are highly anticipated for their impressive blooms and many have a lovely fragrance. Easy to grow, low maintenance and extremely hardy, peonies offer decades of charm, with some producing blooms for nearly a century.

It may take up to four years of patience before you see your first bloom but their robust longevity and ease of care make them extremely worthwhile. Few other plants have such large blooms, a range of colours from pure white, through yellow to coral, pink and deep crimson, with a choice of single, semi-double and double forms.

Peonies will die down in winter, before emerging in spring with their crimson-flushed foliage, appearing to grow before your eyes. Each flower lasts for seven to ten days and one plant can grow multiple blooms. They may not have the flowering span of many other summer flowers, but when they are in bloom they have a stunning presence. So while peonies are generally more expensive than roses, think of these aristocratic plants as a long-term investment.

Peony varieties

There are three types of peonies, *Paeonia*:

Herbaceous, the classic and timeless perennials, produce the large blooms we see in borders and beds and the plants have a bushy, compact shape. These are the most widely grown for cut flowers, and are bred from the wild Chinese *Paeonia lactiflora*.

Tree peonies are shrubby, reach a height of 1.2m, and are the only ones that don't die down at the end of the season. They bloom from early April to late May.

Intersectional peonies are rarer. A cross between tree and herbaceous, they have intense colour with long-lasting blooms, and usually finely cut foliage.

By growing early, mid and late-flowering plants you can have a six-week flowering season, from mid-May through to June.

When to plant

Peonies are available as bare-root plants, usually two years old that will not flower the first year. You may, however, prefer to buy an established mature containerised peony plant, at least five years old, ready to flower in the first year.

As plants are lifted in autumn, bare-root peonies are best planted then, while the soil is still warm and ideally as soon as they arrive.

If you have to plant at other times of the year, the key is to keep them well watered.

Container-grown peonies, which have been lifted and potted, can be planted at any time that the soil is workable, although late spring to summer is preferable.

Where to grow

Peonies are best planted in full sun but some species and the red flowering varieties will grow happily in dappled shade. Tree peonies need a sheltered spot.

Fertile, well-drained soil is important, clay is fine if it doesn't stay wet and they are also happy in chalk soils, but not in sandy as there aren't enough nutrients. The majority of herbaceous peonies prefer neutral or slightly alkaline soil - a 6.5-7 pH is ideal - though tree peonies are more acid tolerant.

Peonies need plenty of water but avoid planting in ground that becomes waterlogged. Don't allow ➤

Right: As the peonies fully open over their seven-to-ten-day blooming time, the loose curved stamens are gradually exposed

Royal beauty

your soil to dry out in the spring as this may cause the plant to abort its young buds; they are quite drought-tolerant in summer, though.

How to grow
Prepare the ground to a depth of 45cm (18") and add about 15cm (6") of well-rotted manure or compost. Peonies will reward you if given a good start in life. They will grow to be about 1m x 1m so allow space for this.

Plant carefully with the crown no more than 5cm (2") below the surface, and the 'eyes' facing upwards. If the peonies are planted too deeply, they will produce lots of foliage but no flowers. For a group, plant about 75cm (30") apart to not crowd the crowns and keep a good airflow. Water in, but don't overwater. They will take three years to bloom well, but as they will live such a long time, you can take them with you if you move house.

You can collect seed from your peonies when the pods are really ripe, but it will take five to seven years to produce a flower, most seed is infertile, they need two years to germinate, and may not be true to form – so it's not for the faint-hearted!

How to grow peonies in containers
Although they prefer being in the ground, peonies can live happily in a good-sized container of at least 30cm (12") diameter for a few years.

There are varieties of patio peonies also available, which are more compact and you could move the whole container to a prime spot to show them off when in flower or group them on a sunny terrace. The flowers are surprisingly large compared to the small plant size and they will need the same conditions of sun and water in good quality well-drained soil that is kept slightly moist.

Use a soil-based compost and ensure drainage holes, and don't overwater. Container-grown plants are already at the right level so plant at that depth.

Deadhead the spent flowers if you don't want seeds to form and cut them back in the winter.

How to care for peony plants
There are a few maintenance jobs to help keep your peonies looking their best.

Remove weeds by hand as if you hoe, you can damage the feeder roots, which lie just below the surface of the soil.

To dramatically increase the size of the plant and the flowerheads, disbud the plant for the first three years of growth when the buds are pea size. This will help the plant to bulk up quickly and not waste its energy producing that bloom.

There is a myth that peonies can't be moved but if you get them out of the ground when they are dormant, in autumn, disturbing the rootball as little as possible, and plant them as soon as you can, they will be fine.

Don't plant peonies back in the same spot unless you remove the soil around the plant and replace it with new soil.

You can divide peonies when they are lifted. Be sure to cut cleanly and to have three stem buds or eyes on each section.

If your soil is rich and fertile you won't need to feed your peonies; otherwise, feed them once a year in spring, summer or autumn with a balanced, general fertiliser.

Being very hardy they don't need any winter protection; in fact, the cold starts the dormant period when they store their energy in their roots where the buds are forming.

Troubleshooting
Peonies require little attention once established. In the autumn, when they have died back, cut the foliage to the ground and dispose of it. Botrytis, or peony wilt, will overwinter in dead foliage and may attack young, fresh growth the following spring.

If you have growth but no flowers you have planted too deeply; wait until autumn and then lift and replant in a shallower spot. Ants are attracted to the swelling buds and the sugary substance exuded, but don't worry because as soon as the buds open the ants will disappear.

Good companions
Mixing peonies among other herbaceous border plants, such as geraniums, delphiniums, *Alchemilla mollis*, lavender and salvias, looks particularly enchanting. Low-growing varieties can be planted at the front of borders.

'Roses are a good companion plant. At home, I have three roses with combinations of 14 different peonies for a long period of flowering from April to July,' says Alec White, owner and head nurseryman of Primrose Hall Peonies. 'Also gaura looks good through the peonies,' he adds.

STOCKISTS

PRIMROSE HALL PEONIES, Bedfordshire MK45 5AH – largest collection for sale in UK, sold at flowering maturity, holds a National Collection of intersectionals. Mail order and open weekends. primrosehallpeonies.co.uk

CLAIRE AUSTIN HARDY PLANT – specialises in irises, perennials and peonies. Tel: 01686 670342; claireaustin-hardyplants.co.uk

KELWAYS – peony and iris expert stockist. Tel: 01458 250521; kelways.co.uk

Right: Roses and peonies are natural companions and make a charming informal hedge or boundary to a terrace

Royal beauty

RECOMMENDED VARIETIES

Paeonia lactiflora 'Bowl of Beauty' – Wonderfully fragrant, award-winning herbaceous peony

Paeonia 'Moonrise' – Vigorous-growing hybrid with single creamy white blooms with beautiful yellow heart

Paeonia 'Bartzella' – Intersectional peony with large, frilly, yellow flowers with a citrus fragrance

Paeonia lactiflora 'Coral Sunset' – Early-blooming, semi-double, ruffled herbaceous peony

Paeonia lactiflora 'Sarah Bernhardt' – Herbaceous peony with ruffled, double blooms, great cut flower

Paeonia lactiflora 'Monsieur Jules Elie' – Deep crimson, silvery sheen, heady rose scent

Paeonia 'Diana Parks' – Early-flowering hybrid, rich red, satiny petals, sweet fragrance

Paeonia 'Lemon Chiffon' – Early-mid-flowering, pale lemon, large semi-double blooms, sturdy stems will usually stay upright

Paeonia 'Albert Crousse' – An old variety with double, gently scented blooms, late-mid season

English Cottage Gardens Handbook 63

Hardy geraniums

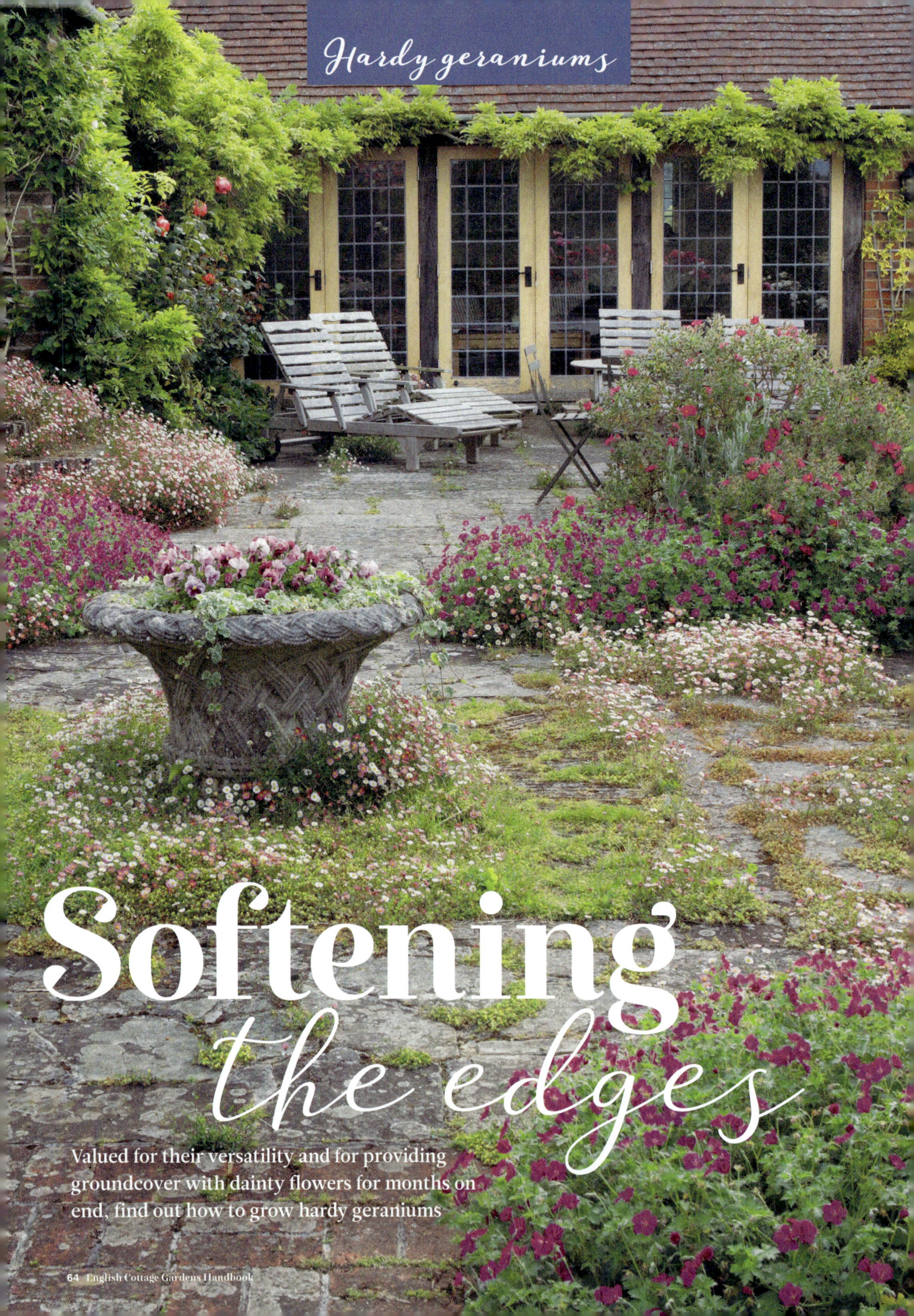

Softening
the edges

Valued for their versatility and for providing groundcover with dainty flowers for months on end, find out how to grow hardy geraniums

Softening the edges

Words and photographs
Leigh Clapp

Left: Geraniums have such a lovely casual charm for edging paths and seating areas, billowing over hard landscaping with their bright and colourful blooms and abundance of soft foliage
Right: Designer Nic Howard plants Geranium 'Rozanne' with burgundy monarda, Penstemon 'Garnet', ornamental grasses and Verbena bonariensis, combining mauves and deep crimsons, to create a beautiful painterly effect

Hardy geraniums are quite deservedly considered the most popular perennial in our gardens, and are among the easiest to grow. Also known as cranesbill, these reliable and low-maintenance performers will grow in most conditions, both sun or shade, and in the ground or in containers. Producing a smothering of flowers from spring to autumn, they are also wonderful for wildlife.

Not to be confused with tender pelargoniums – often also referred to as geraniums – cranesbill are fully hardy, withstanding whatever our winters may throw at them, and reliably popping back up in spring. They get their name from their long slender fruit, which resembles a crane's bill.

Since *Geranium* 'Rozanne' was voted the Plant of the Centenary at the RHS Chelsea Flower Show in 2013, there have been many new introductions from breeders and nurseries. While some are evergreen or semi-evergreen, most are deciduous and will die back in winter. With around 70 species and 700 varieties, ranging from tiny alpines to large border geraniums, you can choose from cultivars suited for woodland gardens, others for sunny sites, single or double flowers, in a range of pinks, magenta, blue, mauve and white, and those with variegated or autumn foliage colour.

'I find that the easiest and most reliable geraniums are any from the *phaeum*, *oxonianum* or *macrorrhizum* species. They require minimal attention, are not especially fussy about their location and are easy to propagate by division,' explains Suzie Dewey from The Hardy Geranium Nursery in Surrey.

'In the *phaeum* species, flower colours range from dark red – almost black – to the palest of pinks; they are vigorous and take no time at all to bulk up and provide a great springtime display, taking over from winter bulbs. One variety that I really enjoy is *G. renardii* – its glaucous, heavily textured foliage is unusual compared to the majority of geranium species, and when the large white flowers open it feels like they are heralding the arrival of spring,' Suzie adds.

When and how to plant

Buy hardy geraniums in pots or as bare root plants to pot up, and plant out when signs of growth appear. Research the varieties as some may spread too much for their intended spot in the garden.

Plant hardy geraniums in spring, from March to May, although some gardeners recommend planting from autumn to late winter to help them establish a good root system for flowering in the first year. It is not necessary to improve the soil in the planting hole unless it is very poor.

Give your container-grown geraniums a good water, dig a hole a bit larger than needed, add in some compost at the bottom. Then water, drain the hole and plant the geranium, teasing out the roots before firming down the soil. Give the plants a final watering in. Seed is also available for sowing in autumn or spring, to grow on and then plant out the seedlings.

Where to plant

Ideally plant geraniums in moderately fertile, moist and well-drained soil, although some varieties are drought tolerant once established, including *G. sylvaticum*, which copes in very dry spots. Sunny to light shade conditions suit most of the readily grown varieties. Raised beds to improve the drainage are advised for *G. cinereum* cultivars, while *G. maculatum*, *nodosum* and *phaeum* prefer shaded woodland areas.

The loose, free-flowing style of geraniums is especially suited to borders in informal cottage gardens, and woodland planting, but they are also lovely when softening the linear geometry of architectural designs. 'Hardy geraniums play a ➤

crucial role in our planting schemes. They can provide dense, weed-suppressing foliage cover in woodland gardens, and we particularly love to use *Geranium macrorrhizum* 'White-Ness' for its dainty white flowers that sparkle in the shade above fresh, limey-green foliage. Perennial favourites are *Geranium* 'Orion', 'Eureka Blue' and 'Brookside' for their early to mid-summer billowing mounds of blue flowers. They will also repeat flower lightly through the summer and show some lovely autumn colour, too,' explains garden designer Nic Howard of We Love Plants.

Hardy geraniums mix well with a range of cottage and border favourites, from nepeta to salvias, and attract a wide range of pollinators, especially bees, with their blue and purple flowers. Plant them along with rows of chives and you will create a bee heaven.

Some varieties of geraniums, such as 'Orion', 'Rozanne' and 'Patricia', will flower until the first frost, providing a great source of nectar and pollen over a long season. Further pretty pairings include with vibrant geums; against the lime green of *Alchemilla mollis*; or contrasting with golden achillea, and they are also useful to camouflage dying foliage of bulbs, such as alliums.

From lining paths, in the front of borders and beds, to groundcover, there are lots of places to use geraniums in your garden. Some smaller greyish leaf varieties, such as *G. traversii*, *G. cinereum* and *G. x riversleaianum*, are ideal for rockeries and scree in full sun.

Growing in pots

Use soil-based compost for growing hardy geraniums in containers and water regularly, as they will dry out more readily in pots. 'All geraniums will grow in containers; however, those with a naturally spreading, creeping or mat-forming habit, such as the *macrorrhizum*, *G. x cantabrigiense* or *himalayense* species, won't create a big impact in a container. You might find better success growing *cinereums* in pots as they make excellent specimens for patio containers with their diminutive habit of low-growing rosettes with a big splash of colour from the flowers,' says Suzie Dewey.

Caring for geraniums

Geraniums are tough and resilient, pest and disease resistant, and require very little care.
'They tend to be pretty happy to flower away with minimal intervention,' says Verity Battyl, formal ornamental team leader at RHS Wisley.

They do not require feeding or watering once established, and will return and flower each year. Deadheading and cutting back are the main tasks. 'Most geraniums respond well to being cut back and refreshed. Not all will give a second flush of flowers, though,' explains Suzie Dewey. 'I tend to be guided by the plant rather than calendar months: if the weather has been hot and gruelling and the plant is looking a bit tired and tatty, that is when I cut geraniums back. Then I give them a liquid seaweed feed and, in 2-3 weeks, you will have a fresh new growth emerging and, in most cases, a second flush of flowers.'

Cutting them back stops geraniums putting their energy into making seeds. 'As you cut back, you will be able to see the new growth already present at the base of the plant. Even if cutting back doesn't produce another flush of flowers, the second set of foliage will look much healthier and neater,' adds Verity Battyl.

Hardy geraniums die back in autumn and regrow come spring. An annual autumn mulch once you have cut the leaves back, with leaf mould, well-rotted manure or compost, is recommended to keep the flowering going for years. 'Any foliage that is left on over winter needs to be cleared away before the plants start actively growing again in spring,' advises Verity.

To create more plants, you can divide large clumps of geraniums as they begin to grow in spring, replanting back into the ground immediately. You can also divide smaller cuttings in April and pot them up until planting in September. Geraniums that do self-seed will tend to pop up across the garden, even in tiny cracks on the patio, but you can lift little seedlings and easily move them to where you want them to grow.

SOURCES FOR GERANIUMS

THE HARDY GERANIUM NURSERY, Surrey, RH3 7DH – large variety of geraniums available by mail-order. hardygeraniumnursery.co.uk
CRANESBILL NURSERY, WALSALL, WS3 2TL – hardy geranium specialists. cranesbillnursery.com
THE ROYAL HORTICULTURAL SOCIETY – information on recommended varieties to choose. rhs.org.uk

Right: Hardy geraniums look particularly beautiful contrasting against hard landscaping

Softening the edges

RECOMMENDED VARIETIES

Geranium 'Rozanne' – Good for ground cover and edging borders, in shade or sun. Long flowering, prune in July

Geranium 'Ann Folkard' – Bush-forming variety grows in full sun or part shade and has autumn foliage. Sterile hybrid so won't set seed. Suits pots

Geranium 'Orion' – Larger geranium than other cultivars, flowering June to August. Works in a border or as ground cover

Geranium 'Brookside' – Tall variety, grows in full sun or part shade in almost any soil. Clump forming and trails

Geranium 'Orkney Cherry' – Ground-hugging, forming a carpet of colour. Ideal for the front of borders, pots and rockeries, or cascading down a wall

Geranium phaeum 'Lily Lovell' – Clump forming, grows in damp shade. One of the largest and prettiest in phaeum group

Geranium pratense 'Mrs Kendall Clark' – One of the tallest and vigorous growers in full sun or part shade

Geranium versicolor – 'The pencilled cranesbill will readily self-seed and spread itself around your garden, but is easily controlled,' says Suzie

Geranium wallichianum 'Crystal Lake' – Prefers cool conditions to flower well. Low growing habit ideal for groundcover

Potted *perfection*

Use a variety of containers to add beautiful highlights to all areas of your cottage garden, bringing rich textures, bright colours and fresh display ideas to your plot

Words Jean Vernon

Container gardening is the perfect way to make small but powerful changes to your plot. Each planter can showcase a single type of plant for a dramatic effect, or a mix of plants to create a seasonal display and longer-lasting focal point. With the right placement, compost and feeding regime, you can grow pretty much any plant in a pot. This means you can incorporate plants with vastly different growing needs, such as those that prefer acidic soil or specialist plant food, into your planting scheme.

The best approach to container gardening is to view each pot as a miniature garden in its own right. Within the small area you should have height, colour and texture. Choose plants for the way they grow, whether sun seeking or tumbling over the sides of the container, the colour of their foliage and flowering prowess. Get the combination right and a patio planter can be awash with colour and interest all summer long. However, there is no set recipe – plant for drama, scent and vibrancy or try the tapestry effect for a softer look.

Of course, plants are only half the story when it comes to growing in pots. The right container can add structure, depth and texture to your design while also making your floral displays shine.

Rich pickings

Most gardeners have an eclectic mix of pots and planters around their garden. For the best effect, group similar materials and colours together and arrange in different heights and sizes to create a tiered effect. If you are buying new containers then think about blending the colours with your home, the local stone, or your colour scheme – it helps to tie everything together and gives a more established feel to the overall design.

'The great advantage of container planting is that arrangements can be changed or added to according to a whim, depending on what is looking good, or the season. New pots or plants can find a home among old favourites,' explains Jim Keeling of Whichford Pottery.

Potted perfection

Whether you opt for productive pots of herbs or showstopping blooms, containers are a classic choice for cottage gardens

Set the stage
If you have some steps, a wall, or shelving, make them into stunning features with containers. You don't need to spend a fortune: a redundant ladder makes a great tiered display unit – move the pots around to keep those that are looking their best at eye level. Take inspiration from the Victorian trend of auricular theatres and use pots of the same size and material to create harmony in your tiered display. 'In my own garden, containers give me the flexibility to let my imagination run riot. I over plant and allow trailing plants to weave a tapestry of colour and texture,' says award-winning gardener Geoff Stonebanks, whose garden is almost completely comprised of container-grown plants.

Ring in the seasons
Flexibility is one of the key benefits of container gardening as you can move the pots around. By planting a variety of pots with stunning flowers, such as tulips, cannas, dahlias, lilies or other summer beauties, you can bring them on until they are perfect and then swap them into the display when the previous planters start to flag.

This will enable you to keep your garden looking full of life throughout the seasons. ➤

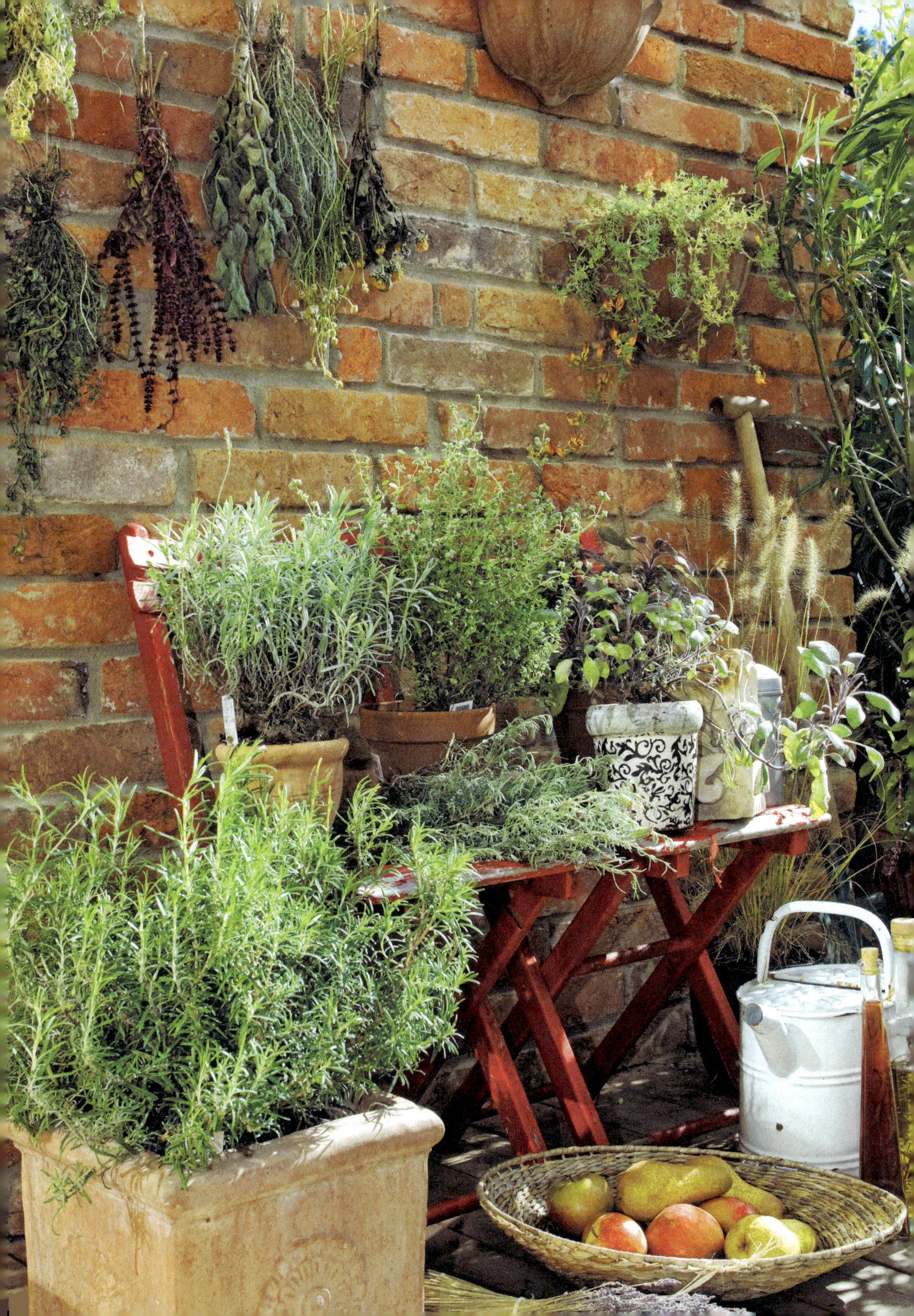

Potted perfection

Cook's friend
Some of the easiest plants to grow in pots are herbs. If you only have a tiny garden or balcony, choose two or three herbs that you love to eat and plant them in a pretty pot or planter. Coriander, basil and parsley can be grown in smaller pots and harvested until you have used them up. On the other hand, shrubby herbs like rosemary and sage will need a larger planter because they will continue to grow and live for many years.

All abuzz
Supporting crucial pollinators is essential and a few pots filled with nectar- and pollen-rich plants can make all the difference. Look for blooms with single petals and open centres as this makes it easy for pollinators to land and harvest the pollen. Examples include borage, echium and echinacea as well as some roses and dahlias. Fuchsias are a container garden favourite, and also are particularly rich in nectar, which attracts the longer-tongued bumblebees.

Classical design
Container gardening is not just about flowers; foliage plants can create a fabulous display too. An elegant piece of topiary can become almost statuesque in the garden, creating a dramatic focal point. You can use a pair of topiary sculptures to accentuate a doorway, or several potted topiary balls to delineate a staircase or along the edge of a path or garden rill, creating a dramatic effect.

Left: Many herbs thrive in pots, and can be a great choice for smaller spaces
Above left: Pollinator-friendly pots around the garden can provide food for insects throughout the season
Above right: Small-scale topiary can add a stunning structured element to a cottage garden

Garden showstopper
For a large pot, choose a careful combination of plants to create a beautifully balanced display. Think about how they work together as well as how they look in their own right. 'In any complex planting, be it large or small, we follow the same principles. We divide the choice of plants into three categories to establish the form and structure of the planting,' explains Jim Keeling of Whichford Pottery.

'First, we choose the centrepiece, which must, above all, have height. Then we surround this with a "midriff" of upright plants of medium height. Finally, we choose low-growing or trailing plants to go against the rim, fitting in below the midriff. In this way, we construct a pyramid of plants. These principles need to be adapted according to the proposed position of the pot; for instance, if we are designing for a spot against a wall, the centrepiece will be put at the back to start with, rather than in the middle,' he adds.

YOUR GUIDE TO
Divide
& conquer

Discover how to divide your perennial plants to keep them healthy, and fill the garden with more of your best-loved varieties

Words Melanie Griffiths

Propagating plants through division is a wonderfully rewarding gardening activity. It's so easy to fill your pots and borders with more of the varieties you already know and love, nurturing them from the smallest offshoots.

Not only does multiplying perennials through division increase your plant stock for free, but it will help your garden to look more cohesive and natural by repeating favourite plants.

Dividing plants in this way also keeps many varieties in better health, as it reduces congestion, helping them to stay vigorous. Indeed, some plants become unproductive after a few years if you do not divide them. In addition, the technique often improves the plants' appearance, as on many perennials the original centre may die as they grow outwards, leaving an unsightly gap.

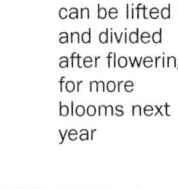

You can divide perennials every two to three years, but bear in mind that it will take a little time for the new plants to establish.

Below: Dahlia tubers can be lifted and divided after flowering for more blooms next year

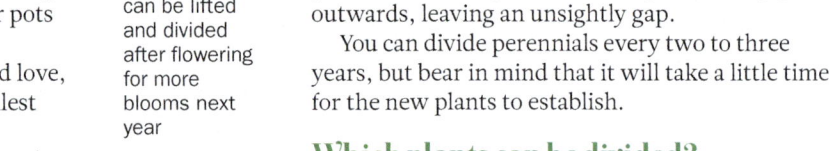

Which plants can be divided?
Multiplying plants through division is a simple technique that works well on many clump-forming perennials:

Herbaceous perennials – the staples of most gardens, these are the non-woody perennials that die away at the end of the season, but then come back each year, as their underground root system lies healthy and dormant below ground. Popular herbaceous perennials include geraniums, delphiniums, lupins, peonies, rudbeckias, salvias, hostas, and many ornamental grasses.

Clump-forming evergreen perennials – many of these plants are still herbaceous, but don't fully die back over winter, retaining some or all of their leaves. This group includes many hellebores and heucheras.

Rhizomes, bulbs and tubers such as dahlias can also be divided once they have finished flowering, as well as many succulents.

When to do it
According to the Royal Horticultural Society, perennials can be divided successfully at almost any time of year as long as they are kept well-watered afterwards. However, for a greater chance of success, it's best to do it when the plants are dormant.

Summer-flowering perennials are ideally divided from the beginning of spring, when the garden is showing signs of new life, but before new shoots grow too big. However, they can also be divided in the autumn.

72 English Cottage Gardens Handbook

Divide and conquer

Hostas are incredibly easy to divide in order to create harmonious continuity to your garden

Spring-flowering perennials, meanwhile, are best divided in the summer, once they have faded and begun to grow new roots.

Focus your attention on plants that have spread out a lot and are becoming congested, rather than smaller, newer ones.

Plantswoman Sarah Raven suggests that you should look for 'large clumps that are pushing outwards from the ground, with fresh young shoots at the edge of the clump.'

Step-by-step guide

To divide clump-forming perennials that have spread out, you can use a garden fork to remove whole sections, without disturbing the rest of the plant – simply cut right down through the roots, and lever out the section. These sections may need to be further divided down into more, smaller plants – aim to create clumps that are roughly the size of your fist.

For perennial plants centred around a closer-growing crown, such as hellebores, you will first need to carefully dig up the parent plant, then use a sharp knife to cut away new sections, going between the growth buds. You want clumps with three to five good shoots.

Perennials with fibrous roots, such as hostas and heucheras, can usually be separated by hand – you will need to carefully remove them from the soil and then tease the sections apart.

The newly divided plants can either be planted directly into their new positions, or into plant pots.

Enrich the soil with blood, fish and bone, to help the new plants thrive. Then water them well until established.

Above: Ensure you only divide more established clumps of plants rather than younger, smaller ones

English Cottage Gardens Handbook 73

Container cottage garden

With a little planning, you can create a wonderful floral container display with old-fashioned favourites that evokes the feel of a country cottage garden

Words Isabelle Palmer

Summer is a time to enjoy life outdoors and in the garden. Even if you live in a busy town or city, with only a small courtyard at your disposal, you can create a container cottage garden that conjures up images of summer days, and enjoying an abundance of wildflowers, meadows and hedgerows.

Right: A palette of soft pastels, such as mauve, lilacs and pinks, combined with whites and creams can always be relied on to provide a cottage garden feel, like here with English lavender, white snapdragon, and bellflowers

Cottage garden pots

Cottage gardens may take their inspiration from the countryside, but with a few choice containers can easily be created in any urban space, too. Most cottage gardens are informal affairs, often a happy blend of ornamental and edible plants that would have supplied the cottage dwellers of the past with fruit, herbs and flowers.

Very often, the containers would have been anything going spare – whether this was an old trough, metal bucket, Belfast sink or a wooden half-barrel. You can recreate that look at home using containers made from classic materials, such as aged zinc, beaten metal, terracotta and wicker. I like to use galvanised metal dolly tubs and zinc planters, which are large and can be filled with an abundance of flowers. A reclaimed onion box or wine crate also makes a perfect container, the warm tones of the wood providing a perfect foil for the plants. If you crave a little colour, then just paint an upcycled container.

Soft tones and muted colours

Gentle, soothing tones and soft colours are the order of the day in a cottage garden, so look out for flowers in shades of purple, mauve, lilac and pink, and add whites and creams to lift the scheme.

One of my favourite schemes uses large zinc planters filled with mauve, purple and white flowers. For thriller plants I use *Campanula persicifolia*, with its lovely mauve flowers on tall stems, *Hydrangea macrophylla* and the feather reed grass, *Calamagrostis* x *acutiflora*, whose beige plumes wave softly in the summer breeze. I underplant these thriller plants with white ➤

Container cottage garden

The pretty planting choice in this container is based on a combination of shades of pink, enhanced by the apricot foxgloves that add height, while achillea flowers attract bees and other beneficial insect visitors

English Cottage Gardens Handbook 75

snapdragons, white dahlias, English lavender and purple *Salvia nemorosa* 'Caradonna'.

If you'd prefer a warmer colour scheme, then fill a planter with flowers in shades of pink, soft apricot and cream. I like to combine the statuesque foxglove *Digitalis purpurea* 'Dalmatian Peach' with *Achillea* 'Summer Berries', *Echinacea* 'Sunseekers Salmon' and *Salvia* 'Kisses and Wishes'. I also include some English lavender, with its divine fragrance that evokes a cottage garden.

Summer brights

Some cottage gardens, however, are a veritable riot of colour, so don't hold back from using hot and fiery colours and fill your containers with summer brights – the jewel box of colours can look amazing in the bright, sunny days of summer.

For these colour combinations I tend to favour more natural-looking containers. A particular favourite is a reclaimed onion box packed with scarlet, orange, dark pink, purple and black flowers above a backdrop of lush green leaves. A winning combination includes the *Lupinus* 'Gallery Red' crimson *Salvia* 'Ember's Wish', soft pink *Astrantia* 'Roma', deep purple *Aquilegia vulgaris* var. *stellata* 'Black Barlow', *Anemone* Saint Brigid 'Governor', *Osteospermum* Serenity Red, near-black *Viola* 'Molly Sanderson' and *Verbena* 'Lanai Early Deep Red'. This selection highlights

Above: The simple flowers of petunias, anemones and poppies create an informal combination that is perfect for a curved zinc dolly tub
Top right: A cottage garden on a miniature scale, here pinkish red lupins, African daisies and salvias create a harmonious scheme in a rustic-looking old onion box repurposed as a planter
Above right: The aim with the flowers here is to create a kaleidoscope of colour

the importance of foliage – the fan-like lupin leaves adding an extra layer of interest and drama to the scheme.

If you want to go all out with colour, then a large metal dolly tub filled with rainbow hues is the answer. There is no attempt at harmonising the shades here, so just choose a range of bright colours, sit back and enjoy the show. We are spoilt for choice at garden centres at this time of year in terms of colour, but the following selection is sure to make an impact: pale blue *Campanula persicifolia* 'Cornish Mist'; red snapdragons; *Anemone coronaria* 'De Caen Group' and Saint Brigid Group 'Lord Lieutenant'; *Dahlia* 'Sweet Nathalie' and pale orange 'Rachel's Place'; *Papaver nudicaule* Gartenzwerg Group and Spring Fever Series; and *Petunia* 'Tumbelina Susanna' with its ruffled pale yellow flowers.

Don't feel you have to follow a specific colour theme. The plants traditionally grown in cottage gardens tend to be self-seeders, which can lead to many unplanned but still wonderful results; a jumble of different colours and textures is absolutely fine. Just make sure you include plants of various sizes, from low-growing thymes to stately delphiniums, as well as those with different habits and textures. You are trying to recreate a feeling of abundance and informality.

Container cottage garden

Isabelle's favourite cottage garden container plants

- **Anthemis**
- Campanula
- **Catmint** (nepeta)
- Cosmos
- **Culinary herbs** (such as bay, rosemary and thyme)
- Dahlia
- **Delphinium**
- Echinacea
- **English lavender** (*Lavandula angustifolia*)
- **Foxglove** (*Digitalis purpurea*)
- Fuchsia
- **Hydrangea**
- Lily (lilium)
- **Lupin** (lupinus)
- Marigold (*Calendula officinalis*)
- **Nicotiana**
- Roses
- **Snapdragon** (antirrhinum)
- Sweet pea (*Lathyrus odoratus*)
- **Wisteria**

Ubiquitous cottage garden blooms

There are so many lovely cottage garden plants to choose from to try and replicate the soft, romantic look, with lots of flowers tumbling together, but in containers. I opt for traditional, old-fashioned flowers that take you back to yesteryear, like majestic delphiniums, structural lupins and tall foxgloves. Add a selection of plants with daisy-like flowers, such as echinacea, anthemis and cosmos, and include scented flowers, such as roses, lilies and nicotiana – *Nicotiana* x *sanderae* 'Perfume Deep Purple' is a real favourite for its gorgeous colour as well as the scent. These are all mainstays of the cottage garden. Climbers, too, with favourites including wisteria, climbing roses and sweet peas. It is easy to grow container climbers by training them up garden canes or a framework of twiggy branches for a more natural look. The flowers of sweet peas are delightful and can be cut regularly to enjoy their fragrance indoors.

No self-respecting cottage garden would be without a collection of herbs, as these were the mainstays of the cottage cooking pot and medicine chest. Fragrant English lavender is ubiquitous, but so are other herbs such as sage, marjoram, rosemary and thyme. Not only can these be used in the kitchen, but their various scents are so evocative, and nothing could be better than sitting in your garden enjoying the colours and scents of your container cottage garden.

Many of these beautiful cottage garden plants will also attract bees, butterflies and other beneficial insects into your outdoor space, so you will be doing your bit for the environment, too, by including them in your container scheme.

The beauty of the chosen flowers in your container speak for themselves, but there are a few things you can do to finish the look. Adding a decorative trim, such as pebbles, chippings or moss to the top of the container not only provides a final flourish, but also slows down evaporation.

Above left: Try various mixed combinations of plants in a cottage garden container, such as large, daisy-like cosmos with roses and trailing ivy, but try to achieve a soft look, with the flowers all tumbling together gently

Above right: Herbs were a mainstay of traditional cottage gardens so include some in your container garden display

Aftercare

WATERING Water more frequently in spring and summer, ideally early in the morning or in the evening when it is cooler. Bedding plants grown in containers require watering daily in summer, but succulents, drought-tolerant plants and mature plants need less water. Use a hose or watering can with a fine rose attachment until water drains out of the container.

FEEDING Compost contains enough nutrients for container-grown plants for around six weeks. After that you will need to replace the nutrients with a general-purpose fertiliser with sufficient amounts of NPK (nitrogen, phosphorus and potassium). Some plants, like roses, have specific feeding requirements.

DEADHEADING Removing dead or fading flowers encourages plants to produce more blooms. Just pinch off the flowers or snip them off with a pair of scissors. Bedding plants and perennials, such as dahlias, heucheras and fuchsias, will all produce a further flush of flowers after deadheading.

STAKING Some plants, like delphiniums, foxgloves and dahlias, grow quite tall, so stake them by tying the stems with raffia or string to garden canes pushed into the compost.

PRUNING Most of the plants grown in containers won't require pruning, but if you have evergreen shrubs, such as box, holly or bay, then a light prune in spring and summer will help to keep them looking neat and tidy.

PESTS AND DISEASES Watch out for pests such as aphids, slugs and snails, and diseases like botrytis (grey mould) and powdery mildew. Treat with an appropriate organic insecticide or fungicide. Remove slugs and snails by hand.

Sweet peas

Perfumed performers

Delicate delights for any garden, sow sweet peas to enjoy the wonderful colour, blooms and sweet fragrance of these old-fashioned favourites

Words and **photographs** Leigh Clapp

Sweet peas provide the scent of summer, and this old-fashioned cottage garden favourite, with its ruffled flowers, has graced our gardens for centuries. Relatively easy to grow, sweet peas have been called the queen of annuals, 'And it would be hard to think of another annual that could compare for popularity,' says specialist grower Philip Johnson of English Sweet Peas and Johnson's Sweet Peas.

The majority are climbing varieties that are trained up trellis, sticks and fences, growing two to three metres tall, but there are also now dwarf bush varieties, growing to a height of 25-60cm, without the need for much support, making them useful for containers and in borders.

When and how to plant

Sweet peas have garnered a reputation of being a bit of a diva, but are well worth the effort, given the right conditions. They do better in places with cooler weather, preferring temperate winters, and milder summers. Summer-flowering varieties are recommended for growing outside in the UK to give the best results.

These annuals need to be sown in cool weather, in autumn or early spring, or in deep containers indoors to be hardened off and planted out in mid-spring. 'Sweet pea seedlings are winter hardy and will withstand a hard frost and snow. Autumn sowing allows deep rooting before the hot weather. When sowing your seeds in October, expect your sweet peas to begin flowering in May or June,' says Molli Christman, horticulturist at RHS Hyde Hall.

Gardeners sometimes make the mistake of keeping the young seedlings somewhere too warm and with insufficient light. 'This will lead to straggly, weak plants that will struggle to do their best later in the season. They are classified as hardy annuals, so will be quite happy in a cold greenhouse or cold frame over the winter,' adds Philip Johnson.

If you choose to sow the seeds in spring, sow them indoors and then plant out once the weather warms up, or you can direct sow in late spring but the results are not as reliable. Follow the packet instructions on your chosen varieties.

For the best results, first prepare your sweet pea seeds. Place them on damp blotting paper or kitchen paper towel for 24 hours, and also nick the outer coat of the seed with a sharp blade or nail clippers so it can absorb water better. Sow seeds thinly or individually into good peat-free compost in small pots, and place in a frost-free spot in the greenhouse or indoors.

When sowing directly, use a tool or stick to make a furrow and bury the seeds at a depth of 3cm, placing each seed 10-15cm apart. After sowing, cover the seeds without creating a mound, before gently watering the soil. 'To protect the seeds from mice or birds, I recommend using a well-pinned-down mesh to cover the seeds,' recommends Molli. Another tip is to soak the seeds in liquid seaweed fertiliser before sowing, as this makes them unpalatable to rodents. Adding mesh or netting will also protect the seeds from birds.

Where to plant

Sweet peas need ample sunlight and do poorly when shaded. Select an open spot in rich, well-drained but moisture-retentive soil, amended with compost or composted manure. Except on naturally alkaline soils, lime should be added to ➤

Right: Ideal for an informal cottage garden, sweet peas add height, scent and colour. Today, there is such a range of types and sizes available, that with a little care and attention, they can provide flowers from late spring to early autumn

Perfumed performers

English Cottage Gardens Handbook 79

the soil at about one cup per square metre on light soils, and two on heavier. Mulching will keep the roots cool and retain moisture while they are growing. For optimum flowering, sweet peas like their heads in the sun and their roots deep in cool and moist earth. They need lots of room, both width and depth, as planting too closely together can create an environment for powdery mildew and reduced flowers. Choose a spot that is easy to access for regular picking, too.

Sweet peas are particularly at home in kitchen or cutting gardens, scrambling up wigwams or string cordons among a medley of edibles and ornamentals. A lovely row of sweet peas growing up pea sticks could edge a path or frame a productive bed in a decorative potager, with the added bonus that sweet peas are attractive to pollinators, especially bees, so are ideal for biodiverse and wildlife gardens.

Obelisks covered in these fragrant blooms could punctuate beds, a trellis backing a seating arbour will create a fragrant summer retreat, and they also look lovely intertwining a living willow arch.

How to train sweet peas to climb

Have your support in place before planting. In the first month of growth, check the sweet peas every couple of days and guide them with twine or clips. Once the tendrils form and grab hold you will need to check the plant is growing as desired. Pinching out the tips of the plant by nipping off the top of the stem with your fingers above a set of leaves encourages side shoots.

'I use two techniques for growing sweet peas. The first, requiring lots of time and care, is the cordon. You start with a single sweet pea shoot tied to an upright support. As the plant develops, you remove all side shoots and tendrils, tying the plant up the support as it grows, which forces the plant to concentrate its energy on producing a strong central stem with larger, but fewer, flowers,' explains Molli Christman.

'The second technique is much more natural: by using pea sticks and not pinching out any side shoots or tendrils, I let the plants develop to provide their own support, which creates a mass of smaller flowers,' she adds.

Henrietta Courtauld and Bridget Elworthy of the Land Gardeners grow sweat peas up teepees made from hazel or bamboo gathered from their garden. 'We tie them in as they climb with twine and make sure to cut them every day once they are flowering to stop them from going to seed.'

Sweet peas in pots

The majority of sweet peas tend to perform better in the ground rather than in pots, however, there are several less vigorous types that respond well to growing in containers. Dwarf cultivars, with mounding habits that don't need supports, can tumble out of hanging baskets or tail over the sides of pots.

'Cupid, available in a mixture and separate colours, reaches only around 15cm in height and can even be used in hanging baskets, just remember to deadhead them regularly. Solway types only grow to around one metre tall and provide a profusion of blooms. They can be successfully grown in large containers (minimum 45cm in diameter) and supported with a small obelisk,' says Philip Johnson.

Sweet pea care

Sweet peas will start blooming approximately 4-6 weeks after visible vining. Pinching out the tips once plants are about 10cm tall will encourage bushy growth. Always pick blooms for the vase in the morning before the sun has time to dehydrate them. Select freshly opened flowers on the longest stems and only cut the side-flowering stems.

Deadheading, by trimming back the old flowers, encourages new growth right into late summer or the beginning of autumn. To deadhead, follow the stalk down of the spent flower to a set of leaves and trim just above the node.

'Sweet peas are very hungry plants; keep them watered and give them a good liquid feed a few times a month, with a high potash tomato feed if possible,' adds Molli Christman.

Grown with care, these sweet blooms will fill your garden and home with joy for many months.

SPECIALIST STOCKISTS

JOHNSON'S SWEET PEAS AND ENGLISH SWEET PEAS – seedlings and seeds; englishsweetpeas.co.uk; johnsonssweetpeas.co.uk
MATTHEWMAN'S SWEET PEAS – seeds; sweetpeasonline.co.uk
SOMERSET SWEET PEAS – seeds and plants; somersetsweetpeas.com

Below: Dwarf varieties intermingle in a pretty profusion, with some entwining around a simple cane support

Perfumed performers

RECOMMENDED VARIETIES

Lathyrus odoratus 'Matucana' – Very fragrant, old-fashioned grandiflora with bi-colour blooms

Lathyrus odoratus 'Fire and Ice' – Vigorous heirloom grandiflora, with a strong fragrance. Height up to 1.8m and spread 30cm.

Lathyrus odoratus 'Sicilian Pink' – Dainty, strongly fragrant flowers that bloom from June to the first frosts

Lathyrus latifolius – The rambling perennial sweet pea produces racemes of non-scented flowers

Lathyrus odoratus 'Alisa' – A modern grandiflora with a heady scent that has improved stem length and petal size for cut flowers

Lathyrus odoratus 'Almost Black' – Scented dark maroon flowers bloom all summer, with good stem length

Lathyrus odoratus 'Kingfisher' – Soft violet blooms with a deliciously sweet fragrance. Grows up to 2.5m

Lathyrus odoratus 'Senator' – Introduced in 1891, an old-fashioned heirloom variety. Usually two to three large blooms per stem

Lathyrus odoratus 'Queen Alexandra' – This heirloom variety looks pretty meandering through roses or shrubs

English Cottage Gardens Handbook 81

Asters

Pastel promise

The daisy-like flowers of asters will brighten up your garden from late summer into autumn and are also pollinator stars

Words Graham Rice

Bridging the seasons from summer to autumn, these hardy perennials with daisy-like flowers add a colourful splash to garden beds and borders when many other blooms are starting to fade.

The first shoots appear in spring, arising from a steadily spreading crown, with stems carrying pale or dark green leaves that are usually narrow and lance-shaped. The flowers can be as small as 12mm across and carried in delightful clouds, or as broad as 7.5cm across for a more dramatic look. The colourful petals may be as few as half a dozen or as many as hundreds and can be white or pale shades of pink, lavender or blue with, occasionally, darker shades. These petals surround a disk of tiny yellow flowers, popular with butterflies and pollinators.

In recent years, botanists have realised that while there used to be over 250 different species gathered under the name aster, some are sufficiently different that they deserve names of their own – although they may look the same to the untrained eye. European species have mainly remained as aster, while American species are now known mainly as symphyotrichum and eurybia.

Planting asters

Most asters prefer a sunny site and, although they will grow happily in a range of soils, a fertile soil that holds some moisture in summer will help to ensure that the plants retain their lower leaves through the season. They are generally not fussy about acidity or alkalinity but prefer a little lime.

Often bought as a potted plant, asters can be planted whenever the ground is not soaking wet, bone dry or frozen. Mulch after planting, and spring and summer-planted asters, in particular, often need regular irrigation until they are established. Feeding with liquid plant food will also help the plants establish quickly.

Bare root plants should be planted in autumn; be sure to work the soil in among the roots and firm well with your fingers to be sure that the fine roots make good contact with the soil. These, too, will appreciate watering, feeding and mulch.

Varieties to grow

There are many different varieties of asters, so make your selection based upon the height and colour that suit the spot where you wish to grow them. Double-flowered varieties have a more colourful impact, and often bloom for longer, but are less popular with pollinating insects.

For bold colour in borders or for blooms for cutting, choose from the hundreds of single- and double-flowered varieties of two North American native species. The New England aster, *Aster novae-angliae*, tends to have larger flowers, while the more variable New York aster, *Aster novi-belgii*, comes in far more colours and styles. These types are mainly grouped under symphyotrichum.

The Italian *Aster amellus*, from central and southern Europe, is medium-height with relatively large flowers, mainly in blue and lavender shades. These are single-flowered asters and are a particular favourite of butterflies. *Aster amellus* is the parent of the very popular, long-flowering and stylish hybrid *Aster x frikartii*.

For pots and planters, very short varieties are being developed with container planting in mind; look for the Crush Series or Henry Series and the older lavender blue 'Professor Anton Kippenburg'. ▶

Right: The single-flowered varieties are more pollinator-friendly and can offer a valuable source of nectar in autumn

Pastel promise

Above left to right: Asters are often sold in pots, already in flower. When planting these out ensure that they are well-watered and mulched

Pale lilac or blue asters create a striking contrast to the vibrant yellow of rudbeckia in late summer and autumn

Aster novi-belgii are also known as Michaelmas daisy or New York aster. All the Michaelmas daisies are asters, but not all asters are Michaelmas daisies

Asters continue to flower into autumn when many annuals and perennials have faded, providing a welcome pop of pastel colours

Care and maintenance

Most asters have steadily creeping roots that are constantly moving into new ground. As the growth expands outwards from the centre of the clump, the most prolific growth develops around the edges, while in the centre, growth can become thin and unproductive.

When this occurs, the solution is to dig up the clumps every two or three years, pull them apart and retain healthy vigorous growth from the edges of the clump. You can then replant these strong-growing pieces to make a new planting.

Some asters also need support and staking. Neat-growing varieties are usually self-supporting, but many medium-height and taller varieties may need staking to avoid damage from wind and rain.

Regular deadheading improves the look of the plants enormously, and cutting back taller varieties by a half to two-thirds in late spring will encourage shorter and bushier growth.

Powdery mildew is one of the main problems to affect asters. There are, however, certain varieties that are less prone to suffer from it. European asters are resistant to mildew, as are varieties of New England aster. Mildew can, however, ruin the lower foliage of varieties of New York aster. The lower leaves, in particular, become coated with a dusty grey covering and will then dry up and drop off. The problem is especially noticeable in hot, dry seasons but despite their disfigured appearance, they usually still flower well.

Keeping the roots moist in summer is helpful, while some gardeners simply plant shorter, bushier plants in front to hide the damage, while still enjoying the cheerful blooms of the asters.

STOCKISTS

FARMYARD NURSERIES 01559 363389; farmyardnurseries.co.uk
OLD COURT NURSERIES 01684 540416; autumnasters.co.uk
NORWELL NURSERIES 01636 636337; norwellnurseries.co.uk

Pastel promise

RECOMMENDED VARIETIES

Aster x frikartii 'Mönch' – An award-winning variety that is prized for its vigorous growth and resistance to mildew

Aster thomsonii – A clumping option with a sunshine-yellow centre and striking cornflower-blue petals, thrives in sheltered but sunny spots

Aster ericoides 'Golden Spray' – A beautiful autumnal choice, flowering through September and October

Aster novae-angliae 'Marina Wolkonsky' – Rich, violet flowers with an orange centre, this variety forms clumps up to 1.2m high

Aster novae-angliae 'James Ritchie' – Flowers from August to October, this aster adds vibrant colour during the end of the season

Symphyotrichum novi-belgii 'Fellowship' – Semi-double and double flowers on this aster, it provides for pollinators in autumn

Symphyotrichum 'Little Carlow' – Robust lilac blooms on soft green stems, it's popular with bees and moths

Kalimeris incisa 'Blue Star' – Striking daisy-like flowers on clumps of dark-green foliage. Prefers full sun

Callistephus chinensis Duchess – Tall with chrysanthemum-like flowerheads that bloom from summer to autumn

English Cottage Gardens Handbook 85

Clipped
to perfection

A craft with an ancient heritage, topiary can add a magical element to a garden scheme on frosty winter days, and offers year-round interest

Words Leigh Clapp

Useful as a design feature in many styles of garden, from formal and traditional, to informal cottage garden or naturalistic planting schemes, topiary can take many forms. 'It is the most useful garden design tool. Fashions in gardens fluctuate, but precisely cut topiary is invaluable in adding the anchor of form and structure a garden needs,' says garden author Marylyn Abbott of West Green House Garden.

The art of clipping plants into ornamental shapes and patterns can add touches of whimsy and humour or sculptural definition to the garden; from flamboyant, fanciful creatures to more simple geometric shapes. As well as hedging and large-scale creations, topiary works well as punctuation marks in the garden or in feature pots. Classic shapes of cones, spheres, pyramids, and spirals bring style to both formal and informal gardens. Trimming plants into fantastic shapes dates back to the decadent days of ancient Rome, where clipped box, bay, and myrtle were frequently used in the gardens of the wealthy. The word topiary derives from the Latin 'opus topiarium', which means ornamental gardening.

Visual contrast

Simple outlines, such as cubes, domes, or cones, can provide focus among relaxed plantings; a single piece in a sea of a wildflower meadow can create a magical juxtaposition. 'Topiary offers the eye something to rest upon while also taking in the more diverse planting in mixed herbaceous borders,' explains garden designer Rosemary Alexander. It is the contrast of wildness and more natural shaping, against the control of the man-made clipped forms that can hold a design together to make a picture of harmony. Take a look at your existing borders and beds and decide if some of the shrubs might benefit from a gentle shaping to create a pleasing rhythm and repetition.

Winter interest

Evergreens make the best topiaries for interest all year in the garden. The winter frosts or a dusting of snow only enhance their forms, while they also act as wonderful foils for the billowing mass of spring and summer flowers at other times of the year. Small-leaved shrubs, such as box and yew, are best to keep the shape defined. Developing topiary from young plants is a long-term commitment, but you can also start with mature specimens. 'The trimming really depends on the plant. I would normally clip them when the new growth gets over 10-15 cm. For those looking for something that needs less care, I would suggest podocarpus and taxus, which can be clipped only one or two times a year. The trimming should be done when there is no risk of frost, so start in late spring and end mid-October,' says Alessandra Sana, horticulturist at RHS Wisley.

At Cressy Hall in Lincolnshire, the topiary has been shaped from yew saplings, pruned over the course of the last 35 years into over 100 lovely shapes

Left: Within the borders of garden designer Rosemary Alexander's beautiful garden, your eye journeys from repeated topiary shapes, which act as punctuation points among the beauty of the mixed flower beds

Images Leigh Clapp; Future/Andrew Sydenham/ Country Life Picture Library.

86 English Cottage Gardens Handbook

Clipped to perfection

Right: Berried holly can be pruned into a statement standard by stopping the main shoot when it reaches the height you want, removing the lower branches, and shaping the top into a sphere

Focal point
Think of topiary as you would a garden ornament. Use the sculpted shapes to draw attention to a particular area; for symmetry to adorn an entrance; delineate pathways and junctions; frame a vista; or emphasise the geometry of a design. Neat, simple geometric shapes work well in small spaces and suit the lines of man-made surfaces, while repeated forms lend an air of control and uniformity. Spirals are mostly marked out and then cut from cones with a central trunk and fairly horizontal branches.

Picture frame
For trickier shapes, you can buy a wire template that remains hidden inside the topiary. Commercial topiary frames are available in a wide range of shapes. 'As the hard design work is already done, you can focus on moulding the stems and foliage into the frame's shape,' explains manager Rachel Orme, from topiary specialists Agrumi Limited. 'The framework also acts as a guide to clipping. Simply prune back the new growth to the shape of the frame,' she adds.

Outside the box
Beyond the usual green box, yew and privet, you can shape a wide array of shrubs and trees, both evergreen and deciduous, flowering and fruiting. Think of variegated and silver foliage, as well as ornamental and productive specimens. 'The best ➤

Above: In this garden inspired by the Les Jardins de Sericourt in France, cones, spirals, balls, and cubes of various sizes are grouped together in a whimsical city of green beside shady paths

Right: Use wire frames as your guides to help create more challenging topiary shapes

plants trialled by the RHS as alternatives to box are mainly corokia and podocarpus. Corokia grow a bit faster but when established they both look very dense and clip very well,' says Alessandra Sana. Variegated plants, such as *Euonymus fortunei* 'Emerald 'n' Gold' or *Elaeagnus* x *ebbingei* 'Gilt Edge' will have you going for gold. Young plants can be trained into standards over a number of years by supporting the stem with a cane.

Topiary forest

Consider creating a complete topiary garden as a stand-alone, statement space in a shady corner. The rich buxus greens in a variety of geometric forms with a touch of variegated options combine to perfection in this shady glade under a canopy of deciduous trees. Mulch the ground between topiary with bark chips to keep the simplicity of shapes the main event. The best mulches for box are ones that insulate the shallow-rooted shrub from soil temperature fluctuation, while also blocking weeds, but the mulch shouldn't contribute to pH or mineral changes – so pine and hardwood mulches are best. This garden option is one for the skilled, patient and conscientious gardener, as it requires a lot of time to keep the shapes neat and precise. Feed and water the plants regularly as their needs increase as they are clipped back and attempt to grow new shoots.

RECOMMENDED VARIETIES

Clipped to perfection

Buxus sempervirens – The classic choice with small leaves and dense texture. Box grows in most situations apart from waterlogged

Ligustrum delavayanum – A hardy evergreen, privet is not susceptible to the pests and diseases of box. Long pliable stems make it particularly useful for winding onto frames

Ilex – Slow-growing holly only needs an occasional trim and works well as standard lollipops, or cloud-prune Japanese holly into curves

Pittosporum – With different foliage colours to choose from, this neat evergreen shrub needs a sheltered, sunny spot in well-drained soil

Photinia – The small-leafed shrubs and trees make ideal hedges and standard lollipops with their bright red glossy leaf tips, and respond well to pruning. Will tolerate most soil types

Euonymus fortunei 'Emerald 'n' Gold' – Compact and slow-growing evergreen that clips well into shapes. Grow in full sun for the brightest foliage

Camellia – Dark glossy green leaves and the bonus of showy flowers creates interesting topiary. Select a slow-growing variety to reduce the amount of clipping needed

Laurus nobilis – With their narrow, leathery aromatic leaves, bay trees are equally at home as statement topiary potted standards, or in productive gardens surrounded by herbs. Grow in

Trachelospermum jasminoides – For a quick result, this vigorous vine will twine through a frame, providing fragrant flowers in summer. Plant in a sheltered and sunny spot

English Cottage Gardens Handbook **89**

Hydrangeas

Vintage *glamour*

Hydrangeas are enjoying a renaissance due to their sheer variety, reliability and beautiful blooms. Find out how to grow and care for these timeless plants

Words Leigh Clapp

These hardy, deciduous shrubs that flower from mid-summer to autumn have seen a resurgence in popularity over the past decade. No longer seen as old-fashioned and languishing in shrubberies, replaced by the trend for perennials and grasses, flowering shrubs are again championed and valued for their use in our gardens, with hydrangeas a clear favourite. Grown in sun or semi-shade, on their own or planted en masse in a border, used as an informal hedge or grown in containers, their voluptuous, long-lasting blooms provide colour in shades of pink, blue and purple, as well as creamy white and astringent greens.

'Hydrangeas are long flowering, from June to October, and there aren't many shrubs that do that. Even in November, when brown and covered in frost, they look lovely,' explains Roger Butler, owner of Signature Hydrangeas.

All-white flowers can be planted for a classical scheme or to brighten a shaded area. 'Massed in one variety, they offer a stunning result.'

'Hydrangea 'Annabelle' brought a resurgence in popularity – designers love white flowers, and Annabelle looks superb en masse,' adds Matthew Pottage, curator at RHS Wisley.

Types of hydrangea

There are five main types of hydrangea: big leafed, which includes mopheads and lacecaps; panicle; smooth; oakleaf; and climbing, with a wide range of lovely varieties from which to choose. Flower heads, formed of clusters of miniature flowers, can be large balls to conical shapes, with some bi-coloured and others that vary their colour as they age. With over 70 species, you can choose from compact varieties, ones with scented flowers or autumn foliage, and even varieties that bloom twice on old and new wood.

Requiring little attention and easy to grow, hydrangeas are ideal to grace your garden and also make striking cut flowers.

When and where to plant

The best time to plant hydrangeas is in spring or autumn as the soil is warm and moist. However, you can also plant them in summer, so long as you ensure that you keep them well watered.

Hydrangeas thrive in moist, well-drained soil with plenty of organic matter, in a protected spot with dappled shade. South-facing positions are best avoided. Most soil types are suitable, keeping in mind, however, that the pH will change the colour of mophead and lacecap hydrangeas – less than 5.5 for blue, over 6.5 for pink and between 5.5 and 6.5 for purple. In light soil, add in some organic matter at planting to help with moisture. Before planting, water the hydrangea and don't plant it deeper than it was in the pot. Water in and mulch.

'Hydrangeas like reliable moisture in the summer so don't plant them in a dry position. Their new shoots are frost tender so avoid frost pockets and protect any new growth. If your garden suffers drought in summer, plant them in semi-shade. People seem to forget that hydrangeas are happiest in shaded conditions and plant them in full sun where they look washed out and drought-stressed in summer,' says Matthew Pottage.

If hydrangeas are grown in containers, you can manipulate the potting compost for the colour you

Vintage glamour

Clockwise from top left: There are such pretty varieties available that look handpainted; hydrangeas are blue in acidic soil, but don't use a blueing agent as it can damage your garden; white hydrangeas are a good option for shadier spots to add some colour and charm; hydrangeas make great cut flowers, but can also be dried

prefer – you can even position the container in the garden bed to fill gaps through summer.

Tender loving care

Once planted, keep hydrangeas watered well in their first season so they don't wilt. To keep them blue, only use rainwater. Mulching each spring with manure, compost or leaf-mould will help them thrive; they don't need feeding, as this will create leaf growth as opposed to flowers.

Pruning can improve vigour; prune those that bloom on old growth – lacecap, mophead and oakleaf – after flowering, and prune those that bloom on new growth – *paniculata* and *arborescens* – in spring or autumn. Lightly prune *quercifolia* and *aspera* in spring, and climbing hydrangeas in summer. Wear gloves when pruning as the foliage can cause skin allergies; all parts can cause stomach upset if ingested. Propagate softwood cuttings in late spring to mid-summer, semi-ripe in mid-summer, or hardwood cuttings in winter. They will take two to three years before they begin flowering.

Certain varieties are ideal for beginners. '*Paniculata* are easy to grow and more tolerant; you can't go wrong with them,' suggests Roger.

In the vase, hydrangeas last about 10 days, and if you dry them they will last even longer. To do this, place in a vase with a few inches of water and leave them to dry as the water evaporates.

Good companions

Hydrangeas work well with similar or contrasting shapes and colours, such as feathery ferns, rounded hostas and ornamental grasses. Select plants with similar needs of soil, water and light levels, and that will flower before, during and after the blooming season. To emulate the woodland setting, plant hydrangeas under a canopy of deciduous trees and shrubs. Mix with other dappled shade-loving flowers, such as foxgloves, heucheras and violas.

Troubleshooting

Frost damage – If new growth has frost damage, cut back to just above the first undamaged buds.
Hydrangea scale – this shows as white waxy blobs in summer, and is best prevented by careful early inspection from spring, tending plants to keep them as healthy as possible, and encouraging predators such as ladybirds. If spraying is needed, use organic options in July.
Lack of flowers – this is most likely to be because pruning was done at the wrong time, so carefully check the label of the plant you buy.
Holes in leaves – Pieces bitten out of the leaves in containers is a sign of vine weevils, with the grubs also eating the roots. Check the plants at night when the pests are most active, catch and squash them, and you could also apply a biological control.

USEFUL SOURCES

SIGNATURE HYDRANGEAS – Golden Hill Plants, Kent TN12 9LT. Mail order supplier and open to the public (signaturehydrangeas.co.uk)
BODNANT GARDEN – Wales LL28 5RE. Enjoy displays of brilliant blue hydrangeas in the ravine, on acid soil (nationaltrust.org.uk)
RHS WISLEY – Surrey GU23 6QB. A treasure trove of hydrangeas, showcasing many *paniculata* cultivars (rhs.org.uk) •

Below: Opt for an all-white variety for a more classic aesthetic
Below right: near-neutral soil or various levels discovered by the roots, can give you the magic trick of a range of colours on the one shrub

RECOMMENDED VARIETIES

Vintage glamour

Hydrangea paniculata **'Diamant Rouge'** – The sepals start white and then change to pink, followed by raspberry red, making for a dramatic display. Flowers appear in profusion on stems that can reach 35cm in length

Hydrangea paniculata **'Limelight'** – This cultivar has large dense clusters of flowers that start lime green, fade to cream, then turn pink in autumn. Best for full sun to part shade, as a specimen plant or to light up a dark space. It is fast growing to become a large shrub, and is very adaptable to different soil types

Hydrangea macrophylla **'Ayesha'** – Domed clusters of small cupped pink or lilac flowers. Does well in sun or shade if well fed and kept moist. Medium shrub with leaves that last until late autumn. Prune to thin out old stems and remove dead flowers

Hydrangea macrophylla **'Amsterdam'** – From the Royalty Collection, it is very sun resistant and a prolific bloomer with large flowers. Ideal for beds, borders, containers and cut flowers. Deep green foliage

Hydrangea quercifolia – Oakleaf hydrangeas have white summer flowers that age to pinks and characteristic textured foliage turning vibrant red and purple in autumn. It's naturally a woodland plant so needs shade. Working well in a naturalistic design, it is a great source of pollen and nectar

Hydrangea arborescens **'Annabelle'** – 'Annabelle' is synonymous with the genus, due to its ongoing popularity. A wild or smooth hydrangea with domed white or pink flower heads up to 30cm across. Grow in a sheltered corner or against a warm wall

Hydrangea macrophylla **'Black Steel Zaza'** – Near-black stems with serrated mid-green foliage, with pale lime-green buds, which open to pink, lilac or purple-blue flowers depending on the soil. Compact and upright-shaped shrub

Hydrangea macrophylla **'Zorro'** – Bushy lacecap with masses of blue flowers on purple-black stems. Best for a cool, shady spot, in a herbaceous border mixed with other hydrangeas or grouped together to form an informal hedge. Little pruning required, remove dead flowers and thin out old stems in spring

Hydrangea macrophylla **'Lady in Red'** – Lacecap with the early-summer pink flowers maturing to rose pink in alkaline soils. Plant in a mixed border or with other hydrangeas. Stems and leaves turn red then purple in autumn. Good cut flower and dries easily

Delphiniums

Head for heights

Quintessential cottage garden favourites and herbaceous border staples, adding colour and impact with their statuesque presence, delphiniums are enduringly popular summer blooms

Words and **photographs** Leigh Clapp

Effervescent and majestic, delphiniums are sure to draw attention in summer beds and borders. These vivid flowers have been grown in our gardens for centuries – their common name 'larkspur' dating back to Tudor times. 'The cultivars we now use have been selected and bred from the wild forms for their uniformity, size of flower and colour,' says Lou Nicholls, head gardener of Godinton House and Gardens, famous for its display of delphiniums.

Flowering early before many of the other main summer blooms, delphiniums will also come back and flower again in autumn if they are cut back hard after their first early summer flowers. 'They are special because few other plants give you such colourful height, and the bee-friendly intricate flowers in solid columns in blues, whites, pinks, mauve, and similar hues,' says Guy Barter, chief horticulturist at the RHS.

'There is increasing interest among gardeners in perennials, as bedding plants have become more expensive. Delphiniums are irresistible in flower, and lower-growing cultivars that need less staking seem more numerous,' Guy adds.

Growing from seed

The most cost-effective way to add these attractive flowers to garden beds and borders is to grow delphiniums from seed.

The best time to plant delphinium seeds is in spring or autumn, when the soil is moist and warm. 'The best annual flowers come from September sowing, where the soil does not lie too wet over winter; but good results come from April sowing, too,' says Guy.

Ideally, when growing delphiniums from seed, sow them in situ where they are to grow, thinning plants if necessary, but module-raised plants are also worth considering.

'The seed is not long-lived, so buy direct from seed suppliers and sow the seeds as soon as feasible,' says Guy. 'Delphiniums will also benefit from some form of support – classically pea sticks were used. The plants often self-seed but the progeny, although delightful, won't always be exactly like their parents,' he adds.

How to plant

Delphiniums require moist, well-drained fertile soil. 'Make sure the soil is suitable and well prepared; they prefer sandy soil that drains well – heavy soil will restrict growth and cause rotting of the crowns during the dormant winter period. Plenty of well-rotted cow or horse manure dug into the soil helps drainage and adds nutrients,' explains Simon Langdon, director at Blackmore & Langdon's, specialist delphinium growers.

In heavy soil, add grit to the planting hole to increase drainage, as delphiniums don't like wet winter soil or to be waterlogged for prolonged periods. 'It's also wise to mulch with sharp grit, crushed eggshells, or cocoa shells, as slugs and snails, who like to feed on young plants, find this uncomfortable to cross,' says Lou Nicholls.

Plant delphiniums in threes for the best impact and take note of the spacing between plants, too. 'Delphiniums like plenty of room – each plant should have approximately 45cm all around. They will grow into the space you provide, and don't like being cramped,' adds Simon Langdon.

Right: Delphinium blooms make a real statement when a single variety is planted en masse, especially when juxtaposed against complementary tones, such as here, with subtle yellows against the soft mauve and blue flowers

Head for heights

Providing good air circulation, and thinning out shoots as they emerge from the crown early in the season, will also help prevent powdery mildew.

Where to grow

Grow delphiniums in full sun or dappled shade, protected from the wind. That said, although they need sun – about six to eight hours a day – don't plant them in a really hot spot in the garden. An area that enjoys the morning sun is ideal.

They can grace herbaceous borders, mingling beautifully with other traditional choices, such as roses, peonies, campanula, and lupins. 'Traditionally they are used at the back of borders, often giving two shows throughout a season, one in early June and one later in the year once the heat of summer has passed. A wise gardener will either stake them as the flower spike emerges, or will grow stout tall plants on either side to support them,' says Lou Nicholls.

'Shorter ones for the front of the border have now been bred and these are also very satisfactory plants,' adds Guy Barter.

As well as flower beds and borders, companion planting a cluster of delphiniums in a vegetable garden is a useful way to distract unwanted pests as well as attract beneficial insects, and they are also a good option for a cut flower garden.

Note, however: all parts of delphiniums are highly poisonous so take care when handling them. Don't plant them near grazing animals and be aware if you have young children.

Growing in containers

Although delphiniums do best planted in the ground they can be grown in pots, as long as these are heavy and stable. When growing delphiniums in containers, free-draining conditions are important, so make sure there are drainage holes at the base of pots, add crocks, and some grit to your potting mix. Delphiniums don't like being overcrowded as they have sensitive root systems.

Place your containers in a sunny, sheltered spot to protect them from strong winds, which can topple them and will also damage the flowers. 'Use a nice big pot for delphiniums, ideally 60cm in diameter, and fill with peat-free potting media. Repot them every winter, dividing if necessary,' says Guy Carter.

Keep a careful eye on watering, as delphiniums do like moisture but not to be waterlogged. Raising your container off the ground will help the water to drain freely. When the temperatures cool in autumn and over winter, reduce the watering and move the container undercover or protect it from winter rain so they don't get waterlogged.

Caring for delphiniums

In spring, protect plants from slugs as the shoots emerge. 'Keeping the large adults away from your plants in autumn reduces the chances of eggs being laid. Clusters of eggs can be seen by lightly scratching back the soil on the delphinium crowns, and it is these tiny 1-2mm hatchlings that do all the damage in the spring. As the weather warms, delphiniums start to grow and the slugs hatch, nibbling off the growing tips, even before they break through the soil,' says Simon Langdon.

Stake plants as soon as they start to grow. 'The tall delphiniums do need sturdy staking – double what you think they will need,' says Guy Barter.

Water the plants regularly throughout summer, and feed weekly with a high potash fertiliser. Use a slow-release fertiliser when planting and then use a seaweed fertiliser. 'Delphiniums are hungry feeders and supplementary feeding during the growing season helps a lot,' adds Simon.

Cut back delphiniums after flowering by cutting the flower spikes down to the ground with the foliage in place. You should then enjoy a second flush of flowers come September. 'A post-flowering haircut to elicit autumn flowers gets rid of the mildew at the same time,' adds Guy Barter.

Mulch delphinium plants in autumn with leaf mould or well-rotted manure.

Types of delphiniums

Delphiniums are mostly hardy perennials, thriving for years, dying back to a rootstock each winter, but there are also annual and biennial varieties available.

The most commonly grown perennials are in the Elatum Group, with the tallest spikes of single or double flowers growing to around two metres. 'These are the classic large delphiniums that can be seen towering in the back of borders. They become larger each and will give pleasure for many years,' says Simon Langdon.

Belladonna varieties are shorter, with a more branching habit and single flowers. Pacific hybrids are short-lived perennials and biennials, looking similar to the Elatum, but shorter.

For small gardens, the Magic Fountain series is popular as the plants are more compact.

'The question of whether to grow perennial delphiniums or the very similar knight's-spur or larkspur (*Consolida ajacis*) will depend on what you're looking to achieve. The annual delphinium very considerately flowers in the first year and carries on between June and October. This nicely fills the gap between the two flowering periods of the perennial but it doesn't quite reach its heady heights. It is also very useful as a cut flower, giving an excellent crop very quickly,' says Lou Nicholls.

Whichever variety you choose to grow, these enduringly popular tall and beautiful blooms, while needing commitment from a gardener, will more than reward your efforts.

SPECIALIST GROWERS

BLACKMORE & LANGDON'S, Somerset. The world's oldest specialist growers of delphiniums, Royal Warrant holders and over 80 RHS Chelsea Gold Medals. blackmore-langdon.com

HOME FARM PLANTS, Hertfordshire. Specialist Elatum delphinium section. homefarmplants.co.uk

LARKSPUR NURSERY, Lincolnshire. Sell rarely available seed. larkspur-nursery.co.uk

Head for heights

RECOMMENDED VARIETIES

Delphinium 'Summerfield Oberon' – Deciduous perennial, reaches height of about 1m in 2-5 years. Needs staking

Delphinium 'Langdon's Pandora' – Vigorous, tall perennial, semi-double, mid-blue flowers with unusual blue and black striped eye. Grows to 1.5m

Delphinium 'Coral Sunset' – Clump-forming hardy perennial with double flowers in coral and salmon shades, May to August

Delphinium 'Mighty Atom' – Slightly shorter variety, with deep lavender blue, large flowers packed together

Delphinium 'Magic Fountain Pure White' – Semi-dwarf, compact, clump-forming perennial, vigorous and sturdy, ideal for small gardens and pots

Delphinium 'Strawberry Fair' – Classic delphinium with profusions of flowers. Grows up to 1.5m and excellent cut flower

Delphinium 'Blue Dawn' – One of the most resilient delphiniums, grows to a height of 2.2m and a spread of 1m

Delphinium 'King Arthur group' – Tall Pacific Giant hybrids with sturdy flower spikes. Short-lived, make excellent cut flowers, and add height to borders

Delphinium 'Highlander Flamenco' – Unusual, frilly pink double rosettes. Smaller than other varieties, last longer on stem

English Cottage Gardens Handbook 97

Small-scale harvesting

No cottage garden is complete without some crops, so if you're short on space turn to containers, compact beds and vertical surfaces for growing delicious fruit and veg

Words and **photographs** Leigh Clapp

Above: Set aside a small area for a veg plot. Plant modest quantities in neat rows, such as tomatoes, potatoes, kale and fennel. Add in companion flowers to allure useful insects

Edibles can be grown in the smallest of spaces, so you are not restricted by only having a small garden or courtyard. Carefully planned, you can grow all kinds of crops – from tactile herbs, through to root vegetables and fruit trees – for a small-scale productive garden.

Shady areas are often a problem in smaller gardens, so moveable containers are an ideal choice to find the sunny spots when needed. Edible crops ideally need at least six hours of sunlight, an open spot for good air circulation, protection from strong winds and with soil that is loose, rich and drains well. Small-scale production also allows placement closer to the kitchen for ease of use, an opportunity to create decorative mini potagers, and to pay close attention to any pests and diseases.

With limited space it is sensible to plant compact varieties and vegetables that can be continually harvested, which keeps them

Small-scale harvesting

producing, rather than ones that are removed completely. So do take advantage of tiny spaces to grow delicious options to add a special flavour or flourish to your meals with that home-grown touch.

Potted produce

Tubs, pots, troughs or even hanging baskets can be used to grow edibles. Whatever container you choose, especially repurposed ones, make sure the material is safe and you won't accidentally leach any chemicals into the soil, such as lead. If using salvage, check if it has had contact with agricultural chemicals or held any toxic substances. You could still use a planter you are not sure about as a cachepot, by placing a safe container inside.

Potted edibles are particularly convenient for a balcony garden. Planting a large container with flowers and a range of crops, such as different salad leaves and chillies, is both decorative and practical. Regularly harvesting leaves of veg, such as chard, and lettuce planted in groups, will avoid crowding.

Make sure that your crops and containers are compatible with the growth of the plants. Many seed and gardening websites list the best compact crops to grow in a restricted space. In general, containers need to be 10cm wider and deeper than the root ball. Shallow containers – around 30 to 40cm deep – are suitable for shallow-rooted herbs ▶

Above: Strawberries and peas tumble out of recycled terracotta chimney pots. Plant in a plastic pot, then slot it in
Left: Everything here is grown in containers of varying sizes and types, from lined baskets and vintage metal tubs to a tiered strawberry pot. The eclectic smorgasbord includes herbs, such as basil, carrots, beans and even figs, sheltered by a vine-clad lattice screen

English Cottage Gardens Handbook 99

and annual veg, as you can replenish the soil each season when you replant. Larger choices, such as aubergines or tomatoes, do best as one plant per container. Herbs are excellent potted plants, as most require good drainage. With fruit trees, check the variety to match the size, as they will stay in the same pot for a number of years before needing to be repotted. Citrus trees can be grown in pots outdoors in summer and then brought inside during winter, and olives are also content in pots.

With all your containers, place crocks or gravel at the base for drainage, use a good quality, rich potting mix that has plenty of organic material, and water and fertilise regularly for the best cropping of your growth.

Window boxes

Window boxes are most suited to low-growing edibles, in particular herbs and salad leaves, and need to suit the conditions that prevail at your window. Planting 'recipes' to try include a mix of different mints, strawberries interspersed with parsley, or a one-stop salad garden with micro greens, salad leaves, chives, basil and edible flowers. Some herbs will also grow indoors on a sunny windowsill, including basil, chives, parsley, dill, marjoram and chervil.

Vertical planting

Cover fences or walls with wire, twine or lattice

An elevated pot of appetising cut-and-come-again green oak leaf lettuce and endives is both decorative and out of reach of rabbits

A small space used creatively can incorporate edibles and ornamentals in joyous abundance, as here, with a standard bay, mixed herbs and salvias backed by apple and pear bushes espaliered on the fence. Make the most of vertical surfaces for growing

Small-scale harvesting

for beans, peas or espaliered fruit; train vines up pergolas, and create edible screens or step-over edging. Étagères, using old ladders, stacked containers, palettes or metal stands, also offer the opportunity for a vertical veg garden. Pots can be attached to walls or you could use one of the many commercial living wall systems available.

Do some research for a system that suits your location, and experiment with which crops work the best. In general, go for reliable choices, such as clumping and running herbs that regenerate after being cut back hard, red perilla, salad leaves, sugar snap peas, edible flowers and strawberries. If a wall is in a shady spot it can also be painted white to reflect light back onto a climber.

Raised beds
Setting up a raised vegetable bed, filled with good-quality soil, is the most common way to grow edibles. Wood, brick or sleepers can be used to frame your bed, and there are plenty of kits on the market. You may like to plant in neat rows or decorative patterns for a mini-potager effect, mixing in some companion planting. Rotating the crops ensures pests and diseases don't build up, and also makes the nutrients added by one plant available to the subsequent plants.

Among the flowers
Think creatively and mix edibles among your flowerbeds. They can blend attractively beside ➤

Above: Build your raised beds to heights that are easy to manage and plant them with a mix of crops. You can place shallower trays inside to plant into

Below: Some crops seem too beautiful to be confined to a veg patch, including cabbage 'Red Drumhead' with its lovely purple veining

Bottom: A trellis can be multi-functional, to hide the working area of the garden while being a support to tomatoes. The echinaceas have a dual role – decorative but also attracting insects to prey on pests

other plants, emulating the traditional potager cottage gardens of the past, where flowers, vegetables, herbs and fruit were planted wherever they fitted. Decorative choices to tuck in include frilly lettuces and cabbages, architectural cardoons, runner beans and peas scrambling up tepees – which can be moved each year to minimise disease build-up – shimmering stems of rainbow chard and clouds of feathery asparagus and fennel. An informal scheme, with scattered edibles, allows for staggered cropping and avoids the situation of feast or famine and patches of empty soil.

Dwarf fruit trees can be planted directly into an ornamental bed, valued for their pretty blossom as well as fruit, and intermingled with roses as ideal companions. Smaller edibles, such as chives, parsley and ferny-topped carrots, make attractive edging to garden beds. Perennial herbs look good year-round, such as tactile, handsome sage and ground-covering thyme with its pretty flowers.

Adding veg and fruit among your flowerbeds has a further practical advantage of creating a mosaic tapestry of colours and scents that confuses insect pests, making it difficult for them to find the veg or fruit they want to feed on. Flowering herbs will also attract beneficial insects. Be sure, though, to avoid space-loving edibles that don't play well with ornamentals, including suckering berries and larger root vegetables.

Successional seasonal cropping

Stagger your planting so there is always something to harvest. Longer-term crops, such as cabbages and broccoli, can be interplanted with faster-growing options, including cut-and-come-again salad mixes, pea shoots, mizuna, rocket and radishes, which are ready to eat from about six weeks from seed. Many crops can be continually picked, including cherry tomatoes, chillies, chard, beans and snow peas.

For north-facing or spaces with less sunlight, try shade-tolerant edibles, such as spinach, chard, kale, rocket, sorrel, Asian and salad leaves, Alpine strawberries, rhubarb, currants, mint, bay, coriander, chives, parsley, chamomile and tarragon. There are many to try. Sow and savour.

SPECIALIST STOCKISTS

MR FOTHERGILL'S – lists vegetable seeds for pots and containers; mr-fothergills.co.uk

PLANTS OF DISTINCTION – seeds for tubs and containers; plantsofdistinction.co.uk

SUTTONS – seeds for patio gardening; suttons.co.uk

GROWING CALENDAR – generate your own fruit and veg growing calendar; gardenfocused.co.uk

Small-scale harvesting

RECOMMENDED VARIETIES

Salad leaves – Easy to grow, great for beginners and definitely taste better picked fresh. Cut-and-come-again leaves will give you a selection for weeks, months even, and by sowing a succession you can enjoy them through the year

Beans – Need full sun, good drainage and are frost sensitive, so plant after frosts have passed. Choose a pot at least Dia.40cm, and make a tripod using three sticks tied together

Kale – Lasts well into winter. Just a few plants are enough to keep you in supply for nearly the whole year. They are frost hardy – in fact a light frost improves the flavour, making leaves that may have become bitter at the end of summer, sweeter

Chard – Very productive as well as stunning to look at, and the leaves are cut and come again so won't leave holes in your ornamental planting

Tomatoes – Sdecially the mini varieties, grow well in pots, growbags and hanging baskets. Plant young plants in May, water evenly and feed with a tomato fertiliser for continuing cropping

Currants – Space-saving trained on walls, or an also be grown in containers. They prefer well-drained, moisture-retentive soil, in full sun but tolerate part shade. Water well in dry periods, prune when dormant and harvest them in clusters

Gooseberries – Can be trained against a wall and do well in a large pot or container with regular watering and feeding. They love a sunny spot but will also fruit in shade and need a free-draining moist soil. Prune annually in late autumn or winter

Blueberries – Need an acid soil to do well so use well-drained ericaceous soil for containers. Don't let it outgrow the space, and repot into a slightly larger size. Feed with a rhododendron fertiliser and water well. They are self-fertile and you could have a couple in containers that fruit at different times

Apples – Select ones that have been grafted onto a container rootstock. M27 is the smallest dwarf size and M9 is still dwarfing but more vigorous. You can also espalier as step-overs, against a fence, or plant into a flowerbed. Options include Fiesta, Discovery, Sunset and Falstaff

Cosmos & Zinnias

A prolific pair

Easy to grow, cosmos and zinnias are perfect choices to brighten your summer garden canvas

Words and **photographs** Leigh Clapp

Two favourite annuals that add colour through summer in the garden are cosmos and zinnias. Perfect for growing in borders or containers, they are also ideal to grow as cut-and-come-again flowers for the cutting garden. A vase brimming with cosmos and zinnias is sure to brighten up any room.

Cosmos

These daisy-like flowers catch and dance in the slightest breeze and are prolific bloomers. Forming clouds of 'pale pastels, bright whites and zingy fruit colours, cosmos bring to mind those lazy, hazy days of summer,' says Sarah Missing, owner of seed specialist nursery Plants of Distinction.

Cosmos are easy to grow and, if they are grown organically, are also edible. Attractive to bees and other pollinators, many self-seed for several years, making them an economical and showy half-hardy annual. Cosmos grow tall, up to 2.5m with their fine, feathery deciduous foliage, and then burst into successions of open-faced blooms, which can reach 8cm across and go on for months. There are lots of cultivars available, from singles and doubles to those with tubular rays or bicolours, plus both tall and compact varieties. *Cosmos bipinnatus*, the most commonly grown, also known as Mexican aster, originates from the Americas.

Zinnias

Versatility is one of the plus points for these flowers, along with also being quick and easy to grow, drought tolerant and another good cut flower that keeps on giving the more you cut. It also lasts well in the vase. With their showy, dazzling hues, zinnias are seen in borders, featured in cutting gardens and vegetable plots or planted en masse for a massive burst of colour through summer into autumn.

Zinnia elegans are half-hardy annual flowering plants, native to Mexico, that stand up happily to summer heat, but don't like cold temperatures overnight. There are many cultivated forms to try, with vivid shades of red, orange and pink, along with soft pastels, green, cream and white. Single-flowered varieties are great for attracting pollinators, in particular butterflies. In addition there are semi-double, double and rounded pompom and cactus shapes to discover, with compact and tall varieties. 'Zinnias are rather fun and great for colour late in the season,' says Bridget Elworthy of The Land Gardeners, which researches soil and plant health through growing, cutting and designing (thelandgardeners.com).

When to plant

March to April is the time to sow cosmos seeds under cover, or you can direct sow in their final position in late May when the soil has warmed up. Bought seedlings can be planted late May or June.

'Zinnias don't like root disturbance or cold nights, so direct sow the seeds in May to June, but not before the nights are warm enough to sit outside in the evening. If the evening temperatures have you reaching for blankets in the garden, then it's still too cold,' says plantswoman Sarah Raven.

Floral design

Plant your cosmos and zinnias in a group to make a real statement for late summer into autumn until

A prolific pair

the first frost. This will also attract more bees than if they are dotted through the garden.

Cosmos and zinnias are useful for cheery colour in any area of the garden and suit a range of styles, from cottage garden exuberance, cutting gardens and wildflower meadows to prairie planting and wildlife gardens. They are also ideal for children to grow, in containers or on their own little patch.

'We plant both cosmos and zinnias with our vegetables – cosmos in rows to help support each other, and zinnias dotted through. Zinnias are amazing as plant partners, attracting pollinators, and bees love them,' says Bridget.

'Cosmos and zinnias are just as lovely arranged in a vase as they are growing in the garden and there are some excellent compact varieties, too. ▶

Sarah Raven's cosmos and zinnia collection is perfect for a cutting bed or containers. From £21.95 for 20 seedlings

I love to grow lots of different varieties, putting together different heights and colours in pots and borders for wonderful layers of intense colour,' adds Sarah Raven.

Where to grow

Cosmos like a sunny spot, protected from wind, with moist, well-drained light soil and mulch to conserve moisture. They tolerate most pH levels, but do best in neutral to alkaline soils and are quite drought tolerant. Long periods of wet and cold are detrimental and can delay flowering.

Zinnias have similar needs, requiring plenty of light in moderately fertile, well-drained soil, and dislike waterlogging. The better the soil, the taller they'll grow and they like some space to spread.

How to grow

Cosmos seeds are large, long and thin and they are very easy to handle. Sow indoors in module or seed trays, covered with about 2mm of good fresh compost. Water from below, allowing excess water to drain away, and then position in a warm place, ideally between 16 and 21°C, to germinate. This usually takes around 30 days. Move seedlings to a greenhouse, cold frame or into a light, sheltered spot for a few weeks before planting out.

Direct sow outdoors once the soil has warmed up. Rake your seedbed area to remove any clumps of soil and achieve a crumbly texture. Cosmos don't need any special soil preparation – in fact a too-rich soil will encourage foliage rather than flowers. Sow seeds lightly, spaced about 5-8cm. Thin out the seedlings and pinch out the growing tips of remaining plants to encourage branching and flowering. Water until established but avoid over watering, as this may lead to fewer blooms, and stake taller varieties. In around 12 weeks you should see your first blooms.

Below: Cosmos add a charming pop of colour to any garden

The easiest way to grow zinnias is to purchase them as plug plants, and grow in individual pots before planting out. If direct sowing seed outdoors, prepare the bed by raking over, check the seed packet for spacing and then cover with a thin layer of soil. Water well and as the seedlings grow thin them out carefully to around 40cm apart. Stake taller varieties with canes or twig supports. 'It's worth taking the time to stake them properly as they benefit greatly from growing straight early on. If they collapse, they will never grow properly or flower as well as when they are vertically supported,' explains Sarah Raven.

Growing in containers

A pairing of cosmos and zinnias make for an attractive patio and container display. Try a mix of shorter dwarf cosmos varieties, such as the Sensation and Sonata mixes, grown from seed, or buy as seedlings and plant out from May, space about 30cm apart.

Use a light potting mix, in pots with good drainage, and place in a sunny spot. Water regularly and feed with a liquid fertiliser every few weeks during summer.

Caring for zinnias and cosmos

'As they grow, stake cosmos if necessary, water regularly and deadhead to prolong the flowering season. As long as you don't cut the plants right to the ground, but above a pair of leaves, more buds will form to fill next week's vases and more for the week after that,' says Sarah Raven.

Water zinnias with tap water, not from water butts as they can harbour fungus. Don't over water, and water the soil under the foliage to avoid brown marks on the leaves.

If you let some of your cosmos or zinnia flowers die naturally and fall to the ground they will germinate seeds by themselves. You may like to save seed from the flowers to sow next spring. Keep in mind that if you want to save seeds that will grow true-to-type, select varieties that have been open pollinated, as opposed to hybrids, which can vary widely in the next generation, and preferably organic so as not to harm bees.

To collect seeds, let the flowers go brown, snip them off, hold a bag underneath and gently rub and shake to loosen the seeds. Scatter them in your garden or save in labelled envelopes or paper bags for sowing the next year.

For cut flowers, harvest your blooms when they are beginning to unfurl in the morning as this is when they will have the most moisture, making them less likely to wilt. Plunge the blooms into a bucket of warm water, stripping off lower leaves to avoid them rotting in the vase. Re-cut the stems regularly and refresh the water; they should last up to 10 days in the vase.

Trouble-shooting

Cosmos and zinnias are low-maintenance and suffer from few pest problems. Planting them among vegetables and herbs, intermingling with marigolds and nasturtiums, will actually help the balance of beneficial insects. Watch out for slugs and snails, especially when the plants are young and tender, so use slug barriers. To avoid powdery mildew and fungal diseases, ensure your plants have space and the soil isn't soggy.

STOCKISTS

SARAH RAVEN – a wide variety of both seeds and seedlings available. sarahraven.com
PLANTS OF DISTINCTION – seed specialist. ●

A prolific pair

RECOMMENDED VARIETIES

Cosmos bipinnatus 'Sensation Radiance' – Bicoloured, heirloom variety; a classic cosmos

Cosmos bipinnatus 'Fizzy Rose Picotee' – Frothy, semi-double, stunning display of white flowers with dark pink edging

Cosmos bipinnatus 'Rubenza' – Deep velvety red ages to crimson, tonal effect, available from Sarah Raven

Cosmos bipinnatus 'Double Click Cranberries' – Bold fully double, available from Plants of Distinction

Zinnia elegans 'Zinderella Lilac' – Lilac pink fluffy domes with short petals, available from Sarah Raven

Zinnia haageana 'Aztec Burgundy Bicolour' – Sumptuous flowers with rich patterning

Zinnia elegans 'Benary's Giant White' – Soft white flowers on thick, sturdy stems, available from Sarah Raven

Zinnia elegans 'Envy' – Unusual dahlia-like flower with lime green blooms, great for cut flowers. One of the more shade-tolerant zinnias

Zinnia marylandica 'Starburst Rose' – First bicolour, mildew resistant, available from Plants of Distinction

English Cottage Gardens Handbook

Alliums

Global
presence

The spherical flowerheads of alliums add shape and colour into borders during late spring and early summer

Words Hazel Sillver

Ornamental onions, or alliums, get the summer show off to a bold start when their flower globes open in May. Like giant lollipops, the spherical structure of these bulbous perennials adds solidity and drama to borders during what is often a flowering lull between spring and summer. Drought-tolerant and full of nectar for wildlife, they are also perfect plants for the modern garden.

'Alliums are incredibly perennial and flower for ages,' says bulb supplier Sarah Raven. 'I love them for adding late spring and early summer pizzazz. Plus, they are excellent for cutting as both flowers and seedheads and are brilliant for the bees.'

Crossing borders

The classic border alliums, with flower heads the size of a tennis ball, such as 'Ambassador', 'Gladiator', and 'White Giant', form balls of purple or ivory flowers atop long, sturdy stems. They look fantastic growing through a mass of soft flowers, such as at Great Dixter, where the big amethyst globes of 'Purple Sensation' hover above the biennial bellflower *Campanula patula*, or at Mottisfont, *Allium cristophii* grows through an airy sea of lavender cranesbill. Many alliums also combine well with glaucous or silver-leaved plants, such as sea kale and artemisia.

Taller forms – which don't block the view of the plants behind – can be grown in the middle of a border as vertical accents, while shorter alliums, such as the beautiful 'Eros' and the chive *Allium schoenoprasum* 'Forescate', are effective growing through gravel at the border edge.

In addition to the globular varieties, there are drumstick alliums, including the colourful 'Red Mohican', and those that produce feminine clusters of pendulous bells, such as lilac-pink *A. cernuum*. It is the more well-known spherical types, however, which give the best structure in flower borders, and that morph into stunning seedheads in late summer and early autumn. These can be left to add shape and texture to the early autumn garden, or can be cut and dried to decorate the house – a single seedhead of *Allium cristophii* ➤

Global presence

Left: Border alliums, such as 'Gladiator', make a statement in spring when planted en masse, and attract beneficial pollinators
Right: Allium 'Millennium' look good at the front of a sunny border, especially bordering on a stone path or the neat lines of decking

Above left: Allium bulbs produce offsets, small bulbs on the side. Dig these up in autumn and replant them around the garden

Above right: Dried seed heads are commonly used for indoor arrangements and make wonderful dried flowers

in an empty vase creates a beautiful feature.

Hardy perennial alliums, which grow from slowly spreading roots, like *Allium* 'Millennium', are mainly shorter than alliums from bulbs, with foliage that stays in good condition for far longer.

Planting

Plant alliums in September or October, ideally ordering from a specialist bulb supplier to ensure quality. Most should be planted in well-drained soil in sheltered sun, at a depth that suits their size: around three times the height of the bulb, which is usually around 10 to 15cm deep, and 30cm apart. Clump-forming perennial alliums can be planted in autumn or spring, or even in winter if the soil is not waterlogged or frozen. Do not plant them as deep as allium bulbs, as they are much happier planted with their compost at soil level. They tend to spread steadily at the root as the years pass.

Caring for alliums

Most alliums flower in late spring and early summer, but some - including *Allium lusitanicum*, *Allium carinatum* subsp. *pulchellum*, *Allium tuberosum*, *Allium sphaerocephalon*, and 'Summer Drummer' - flower later, into August.

Leave the seedheads on the plant to provide interest in late summer and autumn, or cut them to dry them for the house.

The leaves will often begin to die when the plant is in flower, 'so position them behind low growing plants to hide the foliage,' advises Christine Skelmersdale of Broadleigh Bulbs. If the leaves become very scruffy at the front of the border when the bulb is still blooming, you can remove them, but ideally, allow the leaves to die back naturally and pull them off when they are brown.

If a clump of alliums has grown dense and crowded, lift and divide them after they have flowered in spring or summer, and plant some of the divided bulbs elsewhere in the garden.

For healthy blooms, feeding with a general fertiliser in early spring will provide nutrients during the plant's spring growth season.

Alliums are a wonderful addition to a cottage garden, and you can look forward to months of their architectural impact.

STOCKISTS

SARAH RAVEN – 0345 092 0283; sarahraven.com
BROADLEIGH BULBS – 01823 286231; broadleighbulbs.co.uk
PETRICHOR – 07500 937363; bulbspecialists.co.uk

RECOMMENDED VARIETIES

Global presence

Allium 'Purple Rain' – 'I spent time sitting by alliums to see the pollinators coming and going, and [this] was one that butterflies and bees feasted on,' says Sarah Raven

Allium 'Summer Drummer' – A fabulously tall variety that blooms later than a lot of alliums, through July and August. Soft purple flowers mature into attractive seedheads

Allium sphaerocephalon – Also known as round-headed leek, drumstick alliums grow leaves first followed by the flowers. They are among the best for late-summer blooms

Allium stipitatum 'Mount Everest' – Produces globes of starry white flowers that can reach 12cm wide, atop sturdy, tall stems, in late spring and early summer

Allium amplectens 'Graceful Beauty' – A lovely low-growing allium for the front of the border or for pots. In late spring and early summer it bears clusters of white star flowers

Allium tuberosum – Produces open starry umbels of flowers very late in the allium season, from July into September

Allium carinatum subsp. pulchellum – Produces soft clusters of pip-shaped pink-mauve flowers in July and August and works well in cottage garden schemes

Allium lusitanicum – Produces small globes of lilac-pink flowers in mid to late summer, combining well with low-growing plants at the front of borders

Allium karataviense – The Kara Tau garlic has unusual spheres of grey-pink flowers in May and June that appear amid two wide arching purple-glaucous leaves

English Cottage Gardens Handbook 111

TAKE CONTROL OF PESTS

Don't let the unwanted attention of pests ruin your plant paradise – learn how to identify and limit the impact of common plant predators

Us gardeners don't have it easy – we are locked in a constant fight with a barrage of pests that always seem to target the plants we love the most. It can't possibly be personal, but it sure feels like it is sometimes.

Pests can be anything from tiny insects that weaken plants by sucking their sap, to cats having a merry time digging up your favourite flowers. And it doesn't matter if you are working with a few pots or a sprawling cottage garden – all plants are potentially at risk of being ravaged by pests.

The damage caused by pests can vary wildly. Some, like ants, will only cause real problems if there is a significant infestation, while others, like box tree caterpillars, are capable of completely destroying a plant. Birds can gobble up crops or seeds, while foxes and cats can scorch plants with their urine.

But however frustrated you get with pests, you need to try and take a realistic, relaxed and balanced attitude. The days of reaching for a toxic pesticide to deal with unwanted visitors are long gone, and rightly so. It turns out that all of those pests we moan about are incredibly important to all the wildlife we want to protect, such as bees. There is nothing wrong with aiming for pest management – and we give you advice for tackling many common fiends here – but most of the time, if your plants are healthy and you encourage a range of wildlife to your garden, pests won't cause you headaches.

Take control of pests

SLUGS & SNAILS

These slimy customers are probably at the top of every gardener's hit list. Both are easy to recognise and usually pretty easy to remove thanks to their size, although some slugs can be smaller to wrangle (while others, like the black slug, can be huge). They love tender new growth, and will happily chomp through leaves.

Sign & symptoms
If you spy holes on your plant leaves, or just have a collection of nibbled stalks left, chances are slugs or snails are to blame. Look for trails of their iridescent slime.

Likes
Hostas, delphiniums, dahlias, lupins, sweet peas

Dislikes
Ferns, hydrangeas, lavender

How to control
For containers, put a barrier, such as mesh, under your pots to prevent entry. Go out at night and physically remove them – disposing in a way you feel comfortable with. Water in the morning, so the soil is dry by the time they emerge. Surround plants with copper or rough material – they hate the feel of it.

VINE WEEVILS

Vine weevils are a common pest. It's actually the larvae that do the most damage, as they eat the roots. These are cream-coloured grubs with brown heads, up to 1cm long and shaped like a 'C'. The adult beetles are a dull black and roughly 9mm long. These target leaves.

Sign & symptoms
Look for trails of irregular notches along the edges of leaves, which will show the presence of adult beetles. If any grubs are attacking roots, the plant will wilt.

Likes
Rhododendrons, camelias, primulas, strawberries, heucheras

Dislikes
Mint, lavender, geranium

How to control
When on slug or snail watch at night, keep an eye out for the adult vine weevil, too. When spotted, just lift off and dispose of them. If you don't fancy digging through a plant's roots to pick out the larvae, you can buy nematodes specifically for them. Mix with water and pour into the soil.

English Cottage Gardens Handbook 113

APHIDS

These tiny winged bugs may be hard to spot on their own (they range from 1-7mm in size) but they can usually be found in clusters on tender new growth of plants, where they suck the sap. Aphids (also known as greenfly or blackfly) come in several colours: green, black, yellow and orange.

Sign & symptoms
Large infestations can cause disfigured growth, make the plant weak and possibly cause very young plants to die. Sometimes the sticky substance aphids exude can cause a black mould, preventing photosynthesis.

Likes
Zinnia, cosmos, nasturtium, sunflower, roses

Dislikes
Garlic, marigolds, rosemary

How to control
Aphids are food for a lot of wildlife, so keep this in mind when dealing with them. The easiest method is shooting a jet of water from a hose, knocking them off. You could also plant a 'trap' of strong plants who can withstand their attention, diverting them from more delicate specimens. Nematodes are a good solution for large gatherings.

ANTS

The sight of these six-legged, round-headed and pointy-ended insects scurrying about is familiar during the summer. The black garden ant is the most common, which is dark brown or black and 3-5mm in length. Ants can disturb plant roots with all their burrowing, and because they love the sweet substance exuded by aphids, they can protect them from predators.

Sign & symptoms
If you have ants, you will see them. Another sign is small mounds of earth, a result of their nest. If you have a higher-than usual amount of aphids, ants may be 'farming' them.

Likes
Peonies, clematis, roses, penstemon

Dislikes
Basil, mint, marigold

How to control
If ants are in your pots, glove up and remove the plant from the pot over some tarp. The ants will go nuts, but you need to destroy the queen and eggs. Nematodes can deter them, although you could also try tackling any aphids you have, cutting off their food source.

LILY BEETLES

This bright-red beetle is easy to spot but can be an absolute devil to control. The adult beetles are 6-8mm long, and lay eggs between April and September. The red-brown grubs cover themselves in a slick black excrement. Both adults and grubs feed on plants in the lily family.

Sign & symptoms
If you don't notice the bright red beetle on your lily, the fact that the leaves, flowers, buds or seedpods have been gnawed to oblivion is a sure sign this unwelcome visitor is around.

Likes
Lilies, Solomon's seal, fritillaries

Dislikes
They are only interested in plants from the lily family, but they seem to dislike garlic, so lilies grown next to garlic may be less prone to beetle attacks.

How to control
Check regularly, pick off any grubs or adults you see and squash them. The adults fall off the plant easily so lay something underneath to catch them. A spray of sunflower oil on the larvae can also help.

Take control of pests

ROSEMARY BEETLES

These insanely beautiful, purple-striped, green, shiny, rounded beetles are roughly 8mm long. The adults lay elongated eggs underneath the leaves of rosemary from September until winter, if the weather stays warm. Larvae, which are light grey with dark stripes, will appear after a couple of weeks. Both adults and larvae feed on the leaves.

Sign & symptoms
Noticed that your rosemary, lavender, sage or thyme now have holes in their leaves? It's probably due to the presence of this shiny scallywag.

Likes
Rosemary, lavender, sage, Russian sage, thyme

Dislikes
Unfortunately there are no known plants to repel the rosemary beetle but it doesn't wander from its core group of chosen plants.

How to control
As with most of the pests here, the best deterrent is to physically remove the beetle or the larvae from the plant and dispose of them. The easiest way of doing this is to place something under the plant and shake it. However, if a plant is healthy, the beetles actually do little damage.

BOX TREE CATERPILLARS

These blighters are the larvae of a moth and are capable of major damage. They reach about 4cm in length, and have a thin white stripe down the middle of their back, flanked by two black stripes, with bright yellow-green sides. They get deep within the plant and eat the leaves – a bad infestation can destroy a plant.

Sign & symptoms
The caterpillars create a webbing around the box leaves and there might also be some dieback. It can be confused with box blight, but the webbing and caterpillar droppings confirm it is the caterpillar.

Likes
Specific to the box plants (Buxus)

Dislikes
Japanese holly, yew, germander

How to control
Small infestations can be removed by hand, but you will need to do this every day and delve deep into the plant to ensure you get them all. You can also cut out any affected areas. Make sure you kill the caterpillars and burn any foliage you cut. There are also nematodes to help deal with the problem. ➤

CABBAGE WHITE CATERPILLARS

Small and large white butterflies are responsible for these caterpillars, with the small ones being about 2.5cm long and a pale-green colour. The large ones are 4cm and have black markings on a yellow body. As to be expected with a caterpillar, the plant's leaves are their food source.

Sign & symptoms
You'll know if you have this caterpillar because holes will appear both on the inner and outer leaves of your brassicas. You can also see the caterpillars, which is a bit of a giveaway!

Likes
Cabbage, broccoli, cauliflower, nasturtium

Dislikes
Rosemary, dill, sage

How to control
When getting your beds ready to grow your brassicas, insert some canes so you can cover your crop with horticultural fleece or a fine netting. This will prevent the butterflies from entering and laying eggs. If some do manage to get through, remove the caterpillars by hand.

SCALE INSECTS

These are tiny insects, 1-6mm in size, that suck the sap from plants. There are many different species of scale insect, with adults usually having a waxy shell covering them. They can easily be mistaken for a small mark under the leaf of a plant, or look like a growth on the stem or leaf joint.

plant, move it away from other susceptible plants to avoid them spreading. If a lot of the plant is affected, cut off the leaves and stems and burn. Small infestations can be picked or rubbed off by hand, or use a cotton bud dipped in rubbing alcohol to remove them.

Sign & symptoms
Along with the actual insect, you might also notice a black sooty mould, caused by the sweet sap they release. In large numbers, they can weaken a plant or cause the leaves to go yellow.

Likes
Rhododendron, camelias, holly, star jasmine

Dislikes
Unfortunately, there doesn't seem to be a specific plant that repels scale insects.

How to control
If you notice scale insects on a

Take control of pests

WHITEFLIES

Plants in the greenhouse can be susceptible to whitefly. These tiny flies are about 1.5mm and set their sights on sucking out the sap of vegetables or ornamental plants. They live on the underside of leaves, as do the cream-coloured, flat nymphs).

Sign & symptoms

You will know if you have whitefly, as if you knock a plant, they will fly up. An infestation of many flies will weaken a plant. They also excrete honeydew, which falls on lower leaves and can produce a black mould.

Likes
Fuschias, tomatoes, cucumbers

Dislikes
French marigold, catmint, basil

How to control

Whitefly is usually introduced to an area, so quarantine new plants to see if any develop before placing in your greenhouse. Ventilation can help reduce the sooty mould, while a parasitic wasp can kill the nymphs. They must be introduced before a large infestation is allowed to take hold.

COCKCHAFERS

Also called 'May bugs', they can often be seen buzzing around and slamming into windows on May evenings. Adults are about 3cm long, with brown wing cases and hairy white undersides. The larvae can be found in the soil and are large and plump, with cream-coloured bodies and light brown heads. Both eat plants.

Sign & symptoms

Adults will nibble on flowers and leaves, while the larvae eat plant roots. The adults don't really do much harm, but the larvae can cause stunted growth or leaf wilt.

Likes
Daisies, dandelions, vegetables

Dislikes
Marigolds, garlic, mint

How to control

You may not want to bother dealing with the adults, as they don't cause much harm, but the larvae are worth removing if your plants look weak. Removal is easiest by hand – just be careful of plant roots. Birds, especially corvids, love them, so you can use them as feed. There is also a nematode that can be watered into the soil.

MEALY BUGS

Looking similar to scale insects, mealybugs limit their sap-sucking attacks to greenhouse plants or houseplants. Their 4mm-long bodies are covered in a white secretion and they hang out in awkward places on a plant, such as leaf axils. The honeydew they exude can attract sooty mould.

Sign & symptoms

As with other sap-sucking plants, a large group of mealybugs will result in a weakened plant. The sticky honeydew they produce also inhibits plant and fruit growth.

Likes
Hibiscus, citrus trees, orchids

Dislikes
Lavender, thyme, onion

How to control

If the infestation is small enough, you can pick the mealybugs off by hand. Alternatively, use a cotton bud dipped in some rubbing alcohol to wipe them off. A spray of neem oil can also help, as can quarantining new plants to ensure there is no infestation before you put them in your greenhouse. ▶

English Cottage Gardens Handbook 117

LEAFHOPPERS

Leafhoppers belong to the Cicadellidae family. They are just a few millimetres in length, and can be brown, yellow or green. They are most noticeable when leaping from plants, where they suck the sap of leaves, although they can also fly.

Sign & symptoms
Leafhoppers can cause mottling or discolouration on the leaves. Specific species can cause greater damage – the rhododendron leafhopper, for example, can spread a fungal disease that stops the plant from flowering.

Likes
Rhododendrons, rose, fuschia, sage

Dislikes
Dill, fennel

How to control
You can apply a treatment of diatomaceous earth to the top and bottom of affected leaves, or a spritz of horticultural soap can work. They do little damage to healthy plants, so if you can tolerate them, keep feeding and watering your plants so they stay strong. Encourage natural predators, like ladybirds, wasps and birds.

LEAF MINER

There are different kinds and species of leaf miners. The term 'leaf miner' is a reference to the larvae that burrow their way under a leaf's surface. Species of sawflies, beetles and moths all have larvae that do this. The damage can cause leaves to drop.

Sign & symptoms
Leaf miner larvae leave wiggly, pale trails over a leaf. If the infestation is large, it can prevent photosynthesis. If you notice the marks, pull a leaf apart and you should be able to see the larvae (about 2mm long and flat).

Likes
Tomatoes, spinach, ornamental trees

Dislikes
Rosemary, dill, garlic

How to control
As ever, healthy plants are more resistant to pest attacks, naturally taking care of the problem. Introducing predators, such as lacewings, nematodes or parasitoid wasps can help, as can pinching the area where a mining trail ends, hopefully killing the larvae. Try removing affected leaves as well.

EARWIGS

These small brown insects, measuring roughly 1.5cm in length, are most easily identified by the big pincers on their back end. They are something of a double-edged sword in the garden. On the one hand they will take care of aphids on fruit trees, on the other hand, they do eat plants.

Sign & symptoms
Earwig damage can be mistaken for slug or snail damage, as their feasting results in holes and ragged edges appearing in petals and leaves.

Likes
Dahlias, roses, zinnias, lettuce

Dislikes
Fennel, pot marigold, bay

How to control
It's easy to trap earwigs – they love dark, sheltered places, so an upturned pot stuffed with straw, resting on a cane will prove irresistible. Tip it out every day and dispose of the earwigs. Clear up any dark, moist areas around your garden or sprinkle some diatomaceous earth around susceptible plants.

Take control of pests

Dealing with pests
Discover easy, effective and organic methods for taming an unruly pest population

Nematodes
When it comes to stubborn or particularly problematic plant pests, nematodes are a fantastic solution. These microscopic creatures are essentially parasites for certain species, releasing bacteria into the target pest, thereby killing it. Because they only target the pest, other wildlife is safe.

They are usually watered in, but do check the packet for specific instructions, such as when to apply and if the soil has to be above a certain temperature. You can easily buy them online.

Encourage predators
A healthy garden is all about balance, and if you can create a natural habitat for wildlife, you'll find they will handle pretty much all of the pest control. Birds will snack on grubs or aphids, hedgehogs will hoover up slugs, while ladybirds will tackle scale insects. Buy a book or do some online research to discover the best plants for encouraging natural predators.

Picking off by hand
Surely the most straightforward pest control method – and in many cases the most effective. You see a pest, you pick it off the plant. Job done. Wear gloves when doing this, just in case the pest inspires some kind of reaction to your skin. How you dispose of the pest then becomes your choice – we'd suggest moving it far, far away.

Notifiable pests
What to do if you spot an usual pest on your plants

The RHS reports that the number of pests and diseases from abroad have increased in recent years. This is mainly because of an increased diversity of plant products being imported from a greater number of sources. Also, because of climate change, pests that previously would have died out naturally might now find a suitable home.

Notifiable pests are ones that are not native to a country, which could pose a threat to crops, plants and wildlife. It is essential that anything thought to be a notifiable pest is reported, so the relevant action can be taken.

The best place to start is DEFRA (planthealthportal.defra.gov.uk/pests-and-diseases/pest-and-disease-factsheets/notifiable-pests). This page has reports on problem pests, with photos, descriptions of the damage caused and contact details if you need to report a sighting.

The Animal and Plant Health Agency (APHA) is another organisation to report any sightings (planthealth.info@apha.gov.uk) and if you have seen something weird on a tree, visit TreeAlert (treealert.forestresearch.gov.uk).

English Cottage Gardens Handbook 119

Companion planting

Some plants make good buddies for each other, especially when it comes to pest control. As you will have seen in our roundup of pests, for every plant that a pest loves, there are usually some that they hate. So by placing a 'hated' plant next to a susceptible plant, you can hopefully discourage the pest. It is also useful to plant species that attract natural predators of the pest you want to avoid.

Spraying aphids

Aphids are a right pain – the excitement of a flush of new growth on precious plants like roses can be dampened if you notice the buds are smothered by the blighters. You can make your own aphid spray: simply mix some horticultural soap (sometimes called insecticidal soap) with water, according to the product's instructions, and then spray on the aphids. It's best to do this at night so you don't risk scorching the plant in the sun.

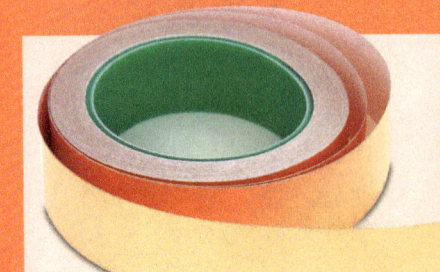

Create barriers

Some pests can be deterred by using a physical barrier to block them. For example, use fleece or netting over plants to prevent the cabbage white butterfly from laying eggs. Slugs and snails do not like sharp objects, so crushed eggshells around the base of plants can help keep them away, as can copper piping or tape applied around the top of pots.

Take control of pests

How to handle larger wildlife

Sometimes a pest problem isn't something you can just pick off…

We've focused on pests of the creepy crawly variety, but plant pests can be much larger than tiny bugs. Here we examine some of the other common garden critters your plants might come up against, with advice on how to smooth relations over. Don't worry – all of the solutions discussed below are humane.

Protect plants from birds

Although birds can be great friends to a gardener, they can also become a pest themselves, especially where edibles are concerned. So rather than watch your tender fruit and veg get gobbled, employ some deterrents.

Netting is the most effective way of saving produce. Ensure the holes in the netting are smaller than 1cm, and pull it taunt over the bed. You don't want birds getting tangled in it. Fleece can also be used, as can inserting lots of small sticks around your plants to hide them.

Scare tactics can save plants from hungry beaks, but keep any of these methods to one part of the garden so you don't scare all the birds. Sudden movement and light give birds the heebie-jeebies, so hang some CDs from a couple of canes stuck in your crops. Garden spinners can also help. Toy snakes at the base of a plant can be effective, but move them regularly otherwise the birds will soon learn they aren't real.

Discourage rodents

Whatever your view of rodents, not many of us want to share our garden with them. But unless numbers are out of hand, extermination isn't the only solution.

Rats and mice like all of the dark, undisturbed corners of your garden, so the first step to deterring an infestation is to tidy up these areas, and block any holes you see on structures. Mint is thought to deter rodents, so plant up some pots and place where you think there might be a problem. Dried mint leaves or cotton balls soaked in peppermint oil can also work, but need replacing regularly. Herbs with a strong smell can put rats and mice off an area – use thyme, basil or garlic as a protective border. Solar-powered repellers send out ultrasonic frequencies targeting rodents, either making them leave or keeping them away.

Squirrels can be destructive blighters, either by eating plants or disturbing them when burying acorns. The ultrasonic repellers for rodents should also work on squirrels, but always check reviews to ensure a product does actually work. Using taut bird netting to physically enclose pots will also scupper their plans. Squirrels aren't fond of the smell of pepper, apple cider vinegar or peppermint, so try mixing some up with water to make a DIY repellent to spray near your crops.

Tackle the cute critters

Larger mammals, such as cats, rabbits and foxes might be considered more visually appealing than rodents, but they can cause just as much damage. Cats can be massive pains – even if it's your own cat – as they have zero concern for anything. So your prized pot of tender seedlings might be their next snoozing platform, or a surface that needs to be dug for them to relieve themselves. Using prickly plants next to ones you want to protect might help avoid any visits, and covering the top of your pots with stones could help deter any digging. Cats aren't keen on citrus smells, coffee, cayenne pepper, peppermint or mustard oil. Use this to your advantage by placing these near plants or soaking cotton wool in the oils and placing in problem areas.

Foxes are lovely to see, but if they are causing havoc in your garden, there are a few tricks to try. First, ensure your rubbish and food waste are securely stored, so you aren't tempting them with food. They apparently hate the smell of chilli pepper and garlic, so placing these around the garden could make them think twice about visiting. Another option is to startle them with motion-sensing lights or sprinklers, but this may deter other nocturnal wildlife.

Rabbits are incredibly cute, but also incredibly destructive when it comes to chomping on your plants. While leafy veg sends them into a delirious frenzy, onions turn them right off, so plant them around your garden. A dome made out of chicken wire that's firmly secured into pots is the best way to prevent damage. Rabbits like to stay near their home, so ensure your garden doesn't become their abode by clearing away dead leaves and checking for any holes under buildings. You could also try mixing equal volumes of citrus juice and water to spray on your plants to help deter them.

Ferns

Shady
characters

Delicate and feathery or with bolder forms, learn how to grow ferns to enjoy the texture, shape, movement and colour of these versatile plants in many areas of the garden

Words and **photographs** Leigh Clapp

Shady characters

Popular in gardens since Victorian times, when plant hunters brought back a plethora of species from far-flung travels, ferns are still valued for their atmospheric, long-lived foliage. Whether feathery, with gently unfurling rolled heads, or large and lush, ferns mingle well in among a range of other plants in beds and borders. You can choose from evergreen and deciduous varieties, in a range of colours and sizes, to add interest throughout the year in naturalistic woodland settings, lending informality in borders, starring in stumperies, adding interest under trees, or in containers.

Easy to grow, long-lived and fairly trouble free, ferns exist across the world in every climate, and with about 12,000 different types, there are varieties to suit many situations in a garden. In general, they like shady, moist, but well-drained conditions, making them ideal for shaded areas in the garden, but there are some varieties, such as asplenium, that will happily pop up in cracks in walls or in tufts on rocks, while others work in dry shade, or aquatic ferns that form colonies in water.

When to plant

Ferns can be planted year-round as long as the ground is not frozen or waterlogged and it is not too windy. The optimum time to plant them in the garden is in spring or autumn to give them time to settle in before the extreme heat or cold. Autumn is good in drier positions as it allows the roots to establish over winter and spring, and the ferns then fare better in the heat of summer.

Instead of producing seeds or flowers, ferns reproduce through spores. These are found in casings (*sporangia*) grouped into bunches (*sori*) on the underside of their fronds, which unfurl from coiled buds called crosiers.

Some ferns are perennials that die down in winter, while others are evergreen. Hardy ferns, which are the majority available to buy, can remain outside all year without any frost protection. Half-hardy varieties, such as tree ferns, grow outside in mild areas or sheltered spots with added protection, such as straw or fleece. Potted ferns are available year round to buy from garden centres, specialist nurseries and online, but do check the label to see if they are hardy, half-hardy or tender. Half hardy and tender varieties need to be frost-free over winter, so are best planted in containers that you can bring inside.

How to plant

'Most ferns commonly grown are accustomed to woodland conditions, which means dappled shade, moist and generally low-nutrient soil. They benefit from the addition of chipped woodbark every year as a mulch, which improves moisture retention, reduces weed competition and depletes the soil of nitrogen,' explains Andrew Leonard from the British Pteridological Society – fern enthusiasts.

Select a sheltered spot with light or dappled shade – as few ferns will tolerate full exposure to sun. Overhead protection from a canopy of trees or placed among shrubs will increase the humidity, helping ferns to thrive. The ideal soil is neutral to alkaline, moist but not waterlogged, rich in organic matter and with a high leafmould content; some ferns will tolerate dry or wet soils.

At planting, dig in plenty of compost or leafmould, as this improves the structure and helps retain moisture, especially in dry shade areas under trees. 'Ferns will take time to adapt, so time and patience is important,' explains Aimee-Beth Browning, horticulturist at RHS Harlow Carr.

Where to plant

Ferns that die back in winter tend to prefer wetter soils in more open spots, while evergreen varieties like it a little drier. When planting a group of ferns, check the mature spread and space accordingly.

Wherever you pop ferns in the garden they bring with them the effect that nature has done the planting. Combine with other shade lovers in the border for a lush foliage display, or edging pathways. Companion planting ferns with hostas, epimedium, astilbe, dicentra, galanthus, polygonatum and cyclamen allows you to play with colours and textures. 'Ferns are great for adding shape and texture, while also providing a wonderful backdrop for other plants. Drought tolerant ferns, such as *Dryopteris filix-mas*, asplenium, and *Polystichum setiferum* are great choices for a tricky, shady spot. Hellebores, bleeding heart, *Anemone nemorosa* 'Allenii', ➤

Left: Unfurling shuttlecock ferns with their astringent green fronds interspersed with bulbs of blue and mauve, such as squill and bluebells, are one of the seasonal delights to savour *Right:* The dwarf evergreen fern, *Polystichum setiferum*, is an ancient species and is a great survivor that will tolerate dry, shady conditions

Above: For containers, use ferns that are small in size, some of which will happily colonise in cracks in walls as well, such as asplenium, blechnum and dryopteris

Milium effusum 'Aureum' and daffodils make perfect spring companions. For autumn colour, add *Liriope muscari*, colchicum and Japanese anemones,' suggests Asa Gregers-Warg, head gardener at the Beth Chatto Gardens.

For a year-round display under tree canopies, use wintergreen rather than deciduous ferns, these are also more drought tolerant. Ferns are natural along watercourses as most prefer a damp soil, so mix them in with primulas and other marginals around a pond or stream. 'The Royal fern, *Osmunda regalis* will make a stunning focal point near a pond or stream where the soil is constantly moist. Forming a tall, elegant clump, its unfolding fronds carry a tint of copper before becoming green, until autumn when they turn a lovely rusty-brown. Add *Leucojum aestivum* 'Gravetye Giant' for spring interest, while astilbe, hosta and *Iris sibirica* are ideal partners through the summer months,' adds Asa Gregers-Warg.

Many ferns are ideal for rockeries or peeping out of dry stone walls for an aged and natural feel. 'I do love polypodiums. I try to mimic how they grow out in the wild, where you can find them growing on tree branches and walls that have collected organic matter over time to nurture the fern. The rhizome just creeps along using the surface for support. *P. vulgare* and *P. cambricum* have some amazing cultivars that are feathery and elegant,' says Aimee-Beth Browning.

Consider planting a naturalistic collection of ferns in a stumpery. 'A shady, damp area lends itself best for the position of a stumpery. The format is to plant the stumps and surrounding areas densely so as to envelop and complement the stumps themselves. Exposed soil is minimal, which in turn reduces weed growth, so this is a low maintenance option. A good layer of leafmould prior to planting is essential and some ferns will need feeding, especially those planted in small pockets within the stumps. Use hardwood only as softwood will degrade too readily,' explains David Perry, garden manager at RHS Garden Rosemoor.

Growing ferns in pots

Shallow rooted, all ferns are suitable for growing in containers, and the attractive foliage, ranging from greens through silver, burgundy and bronze, offers many creative combinations. Ferns require moist conditions, so water potted plants regularly to keep the soil just moist and add a general fertiliser during the growing season. Pots can be moved giving you a lot of scope for selecting the perfect spot and creating groupings, from a mini-fernery effect to mixed plantings with other shade-lovers.

You can tailor the growing conditions to suit the particular ferns you choose, and they are also suitable for hanging baskets or vertical gardens.

How to care for ferns

To propagate ferns, divide clumps and replant in spring. 'Ferns are very adaptable and it takes a bit of time to see the results of your nurturing, but they have been around for centuries and are very resilient,' advises Aimee-Beth Browning.

Water newly planted ferns regularly for their first year, and through periods of drought – soaking the roots rather than on the fronds to avoid foliage rotting. Top up the mulch each spring to help water retention and enrich the soil.

Tree ferns will benefit from a monthly liquid feed applied to their trunks from spring to early summer, or a scattering of controlled-release fertiliser at the base each spring, along with a misting of water on the trunk to keep them damp.

FERN NURSERIES

CRAWFORD FERNS, Spetisbury, Dorset DT11 9DP – over 100 fern varieties. crawfordferns.co.uk
THE FERN NURSERY, Binbrook, Lincolnshire LN8 6DH – 80 to 100 hardy native and foreign ferns and tree ferns. fernnursery.co.uk
FIBREX NURSERIES, Stratford-upon-Avon, Warwickshire CV37 8XP – over 200 fern types, hardy, native and foreign tender. fibrex.co.uk
LONG ACRE PLANTS, Wincanton, Somerset BA9 8EX – nearly 100 hardy native and foreign varieties of ferns to choose from. plantsforshade.co.uk

Shady characters

RECOMMENDED VARIETIES

Matteuccia struthiopteris – A deciduous slow-growing fern that forms colonies of attractive rosettes

Tree ferns – Originate from Australia and are tropical and exotic-looking. Easy to grow, they need a sheltered position and winter protection

Dryopteris erythrosora 'Brilliance' – Bronze new fronds in spring, green in summer, orange-red autumn spores

Polypodium vulgare – An evergreen UK native, grows to 0.5m with a 1m spread, in full sun to part shade

Adiantum venustum – Himalayan maidenhair, is a deciduous fern, with fresh green spring growth and shiny black stalks. Adds a light, airy texture

Polystichum polyblepharum – Evergreen Japanese lace fern, has very stiff, erect fronds. Ideal for year-round interest

Adiantum pedatum – Or five-fingered maidenhair, is a clump-forming, hardy deciduous fern

Blechnum brasiliense 'Volcano' – Also known as the dwarf Brazilian tree fern. Use this evergreen for an exotic garden, in patio containers or under glass

Arachnoides aristata 'Variegata' – East Indian holly fern fronds die back in autumn. Protect from the cold

English Cottage Gardens Handbook **125**

Dahlias

Dazzling delights

These showy flowers make an invaluable addition to gardens, gracing them with their flamboyant blooms in myriad shapes and colours from June right through to December

Words and **photographs** Leigh Clapp

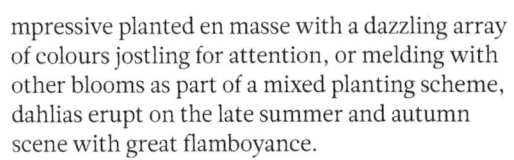

Impressive planted en masse with a dazzling array of colours jostling for attention, or melding with other blooms as part of a mixed planting scheme, dahlias erupt on the late summer and autumn scene with great flamboyance.

A member of the asteraceae family, there are around 36 species of dahlias, with thousands of various cultivars and hybrids. Skilled breeders across the world have produced a wide range of sizes and colours, practically unmatched in the world of flowers. Dahlias can be described as decorative, cactus, anemone, waterlily, pompon, balls, collarette, dwarf, peony or orchid. Sizes range from the smallest lilliput to dinnerplate-sized blooms, while there is every colour except for blue – that most elusive hue for breeders.

A potted history

Dahlias originate from the mountains of Mexico, Columbia and Guatemala and were first recorded by westerners in 1615. They are named after the Swedish botanist, Dr Anders Dahl, who originally regarded them as a vegetable rather than a garden flower. Their beauty has been much admired since the development of varieties with large, double blooms were bred in Belgium in 1815. In a few short years, nearly every colour that we know today had been introduced and there were hundreds listed in catalogues for plant-obsessed gardeners of the era.

Design changes

There is a sense of nostalgia with dahlias: once everyone grew them, often in rows among the vegetables or as brassy displays in gardens, before fashions changed and they began to fall out of favour. Garden designers, such as Beth Chatto in the 1970s, and Piet Oudolf in the 1990s, brought more subtle, natural-looking designs to the fore. Breeders started developing dahlia varieties for modern planting schemes, with daintier sizes that melded into planting combinations of grasses and perennials. A new wave saw great popularity of dark foliaged dahlias, such as the 'Bishop of Llandaff' and 'David Howard', while a resurgence for bright, cheering colours has also seen seas of dahlias mass-planted as a crescendo to the season.

Dazzling delights

Grow your favourite colour combinations and styles of dahlia together, staking the ones with larger blooms, but also planting them fairly close together so that they can help support each other

Above: A mix of open flowering single and semi-double dahlias, such as here with candy pink 'Hartenaas', white 'Bishop of Dover' and crimson 'Bishop of Auckland', are best for pollinators as the eye of the flower is exposed, enabling the insects to easily land and reach for the sweet nectar

Planting practicalities

It is important that you prepare the soil well for these hungry plants.
- They need a sunny spot, protected from strong winds, in rich, moist, well-drained and loamy soil but not wet, waterlogged soils.
- Plant tubers once frosts have passed, allowing about eight weeks to the start of flowering.
- Select varieties for your weather conditions and by the shape, size and colour. Tubers can be purchased through mail order, in packets at nurseries, or you may be able to scrounge some from a kind friend who has divided their clump of tubers. Ensure that each piece has some stem and at least one of the buds or 'eyes'.
- Dig a hole about 30cm deep, add in some compost or manure and wet with a watering can of water. Don't divide the roots prior to planting, and position the tubers about 10 to 12cm deep with the crowns pointing up, spaced about 75cm apart, depending on the variety.
- Tall-growing dahlias will need staking and it is a good idea to position the stake at planting. Unless the soil is very dry, don't water the plants until they have grown about 15cm high, to avoid the tuber rotting. As they grow, pinch out the growing tips to promote bushy growth.
- Protect them from slugs and snails and deadhead regularly to keep the plant flowering.
- After the season is finished, cut back to ground level, mulch deeply if leaving in the ground in mild areas, or lift the tubers, clean them and leave to dry, then wrap them in newspaper or in wood shavings and store somewhere frost and damp free.
- In very free-draining soil, leave the stems to go black from the first frost for approximately a fortnight to allow the sugars to go back down the stems to feed the tuber. Then cut the stems off just below ground level, mound up the soil or add compost to protect the tuber over winter.
- In poorly drained or clay soil, at the first frost cut them down by half and then lift the tubers.
- When planting dahlias in containers, choose a pot that is at least 30cm in diameter, use a good, multi-purpose compost and add a slow-release fertiliser. Be careful not to let them dry out and some will need staking. There are some diminutive varieties perfect for pots, such as dwarf colarettes, lilyputs and the low-growing Topmix series.

Complementary combinations

Dahlias work well mixed with other robust perennials in a bed or border, happily mingling with contrasting opulent autumnal plants or blending the tones for harmonious effects. Combine them in communities of plants that like similar conditions. Most grow to large bushes, so taller plants, such as eupatorium, agapanthus and buddleias work as a backdrop and ensure any smaller foreground plants can cope with being shaded by their leaves.

Their companion plants can be the perfect accent to set them off or aid in deterring pests from their blooms. Some can do double duty of complementing and preventing pests, such as artemisia, fennel, salvias and nasturtium. Hot borders sing with red dahlias against clouds of fennel, burnished sunflowers, clumps of bright orange spires of kniphofias, and stripy cannas, cooled by splashes of blue salvias, for example. Other great border companions include ornamental grasses as a foil to their flamboyance, *Verbena bonariensis*, crocosmias, heleniums, agastache, rudbeckias and persicarias.

Open-centred single and semi-double varieties that produce an array of simple flowers are the best choice for pollinators as they can see where to land and feed on the nectar, and look charming mingling with asters and other daisy-shaped flowers.

In a cutting garden, decorative and cactus dahlias, in particular, are the ideal cut-and-come-again blooms, flowering for months on end. Picking them regularly encourages more to flower right up to the first frosts. Recut the stems under water and they last in a vase for four to six days.

SPECIALIST GROWERS

GILBERTS NURSERY – Sherfield English, Hampshire, SO51 6DT. Dahlia field open mid August to October (gilbertsdahlias.co.uk)
AYLETT NURSERIES – St Albans, Herts, AL2 1DH (Tel: 01727 822255; aylettnurseries.co.uk)
HARTS NURSERY – Congleton, Cheshire, CW12 4TG (Tel: 07855 785540; hartsnursery.co.uk)

Dazzling delights

RECOMMENDED VARIETIES

Dahlia 'Bishop of Llandaff' – This peony-flowered dahlia has vermilion flowers on dark foliage. It dies back in autumn, with fresh, new growth in spring

Dahlia 'David Howard' – An impressive, decorative dahlia that is lovely in borders with its profuse burnished orange blooms on chocolate foliage. It has more flowers over a longer period than many dahlias, making it one of the most popular

Dahlia 'Totally Tangerine' – An anemone type, blending orange and pink tones with outer petals and inner tubular florets. It is great for containers, in borders and as a cut flower

Dahlia 'Honka Surprise' – An orchid type with unique star-shaped pink petals and yellow centre. Its compact size works at the front of borders and in containers

Dahlia 'Fashion Monger' – Looks lovely in a vase, the border and in containers with its splash of colour on a white base. Originally introduced in 1955, this colarette variety has a charming retro feel

Dahlia 'Blackberry Ripple' – Sounds delicious and looks delicious with splashes and drizzles of crimson and purple. Position this semi-cactus variety in the border with similar tones

Dahlia 'Chilson's Pride' – An informal decorative dahlia, has softly pretty pink petals around a pale cream centre that blends in a harmonious border scheme, and is an equally lovely cut flower

Dahlia 'Crossfield Ebony' – A pompon variety, has a steady stream of delightful, darkly maroon spheres, ideal for the vase and in a mixed border. The small size of the flowers works attractively mingling with a cottage-styled border

Dahlia 'Babylon Purple' – With its purple and red dinner-plate blooms held on long stems, is stunning planted en masse with dark leafed plants, and also makes an exceptional cutting flower

The English Cottage GARDEN handbook

Future PLC Quay House, The Ambury, Bath, BA1 1UA

Bookazine Editorial
Group Editor **Philippa Grafton**
Art Editor **Lora Barnes**
Head of Art & Design **Greg Whitaker**
Editorial Director **Jon White**
Managing Director **Grainne McKenna**

Period Living Editorial
Editor **Rachel Crow**
Group Art Director **Alison Walker**

Cover images
Alamy and Getty

Photography
All copyrights and trademarks are recognised and respected

Advertising
Media packs are available on request
Commercial Director **Clare Dove**

International
Head of Print Licensing **Rachel Shaw**
licensing@futurenet.com
www.futurecontenthub.com

Circulation
Head of Newstrade **Tim Mathers**

Production
Head of Production **Mark Constance**
Production Project Manager **Matthew Eglinton**
Advertising Production Manager **Joanne Crosby**
Digital Editions Controller **Jason Hudson**
Production Managers **Keely Miller, Nola Cokely, Vivienne Calvert, Fran Twentyman**

Printed in the UK

Distributed by Marketforce – www.marketforce.co.uk
For enquiries, please email: mfcommunications@futurenet.com

English Cottage Garden Handbook First Edition (HOB5773)
© 2024 Future Publishing Limited

We are committed to only using magazine paper which is derived from responsibly managed, certified forestry and chlorine-free manufacture. The paper in this bookazine was sourced and produced from sustainable managed forests, conforming to strict environmental and socioeconomic standards.

All contents © 2024 Future Publishing Limited or published under licence. All rights reserved. No part of this magazine may be used, stored, transmitted or reproduced in any way without the prior written permission of the publisher. Future Publishing Limited (company number 2008885) is registered in England and Wales. Registered office: Quay House, The Ambury, Bath BA1 1UA. All information contained in this publication is for information only and is, as far as we are aware, correct at the time of going to press. Future cannot accept any responsibility for errors or inaccuracies in such information. You are advised to contact manufacturers and retailers directly with regard to the price of products/services referred to in this publication. Apps and websites mentioned in this publication are not under our control. We are not responsible for their contents or any other changes or updates to them. This magazine is fully independent and not affiliated in any way with the companies mentioned herein.

FUTURE Connectors. Creators. Experience Makers.

Future plc is a public company quoted on the London Stock Exchange (symbol: FUTR)
www.futureplc.com

Chief Executive Officer **Jon Steinberg**
Non-Executive Chairman **Richard Huntingford**
Chief Financial and Strategy Officer **Penny Ladkin-Brand**

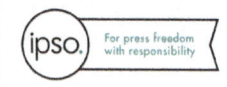

Tel +44 (0)1225 442 244

Widely Recycled

ipso. For press freedom with responsibility

Printed in Dunstable, United Kingdom